ALPHABET PRAYERS

The POWER of PRAYING SCRIPTURE into the HEARTS YOU LOVE...

For Your Husband, Children & Pastor

by Tammy M. Price

VMI PUBLISHERS

Partnering With Christian Authors, Publishing Christian and Inspirational Books

Sisters, OR

Published by

a division of VMI Publishers
Sisters, Oregon
www.vmipublishers.com

ISBN 1-933204-10-9
ISBN 13: 978-1-933204-10-9

Library of Congress Control Number: 2005932425

Author Contact:
HOPministries03@aol.com
www.heartsofprayer.com

DEDICATION

With all glory to God, this book is dedicated to all those who have faithfully prayed, encouraged, and helped me to press on towards the goal. To Donnie, my wonderful husband and partner in Christ, who handed me a notebook and his pen one Sunday afternoon and said, "That's the best idea you've ever had, sweetie — write a book!" I praise God for you every day, and could not have done this without you! I also praise God for my five precious children: CJ, JD, Ali, DJ and MJ, as well all my family who have loved me, especially through the rough spots! A special thank-you to my pastor Julian Riddle and his wife Debbie for their godly teaching, encouragement, caring, and the example they set for all who are watching!

I would also like to make special mention of a dear friend and especially faithful prayer partner, Melissa Johnson, who has been a true inspiration and godly example of allowing God's love to flow through a forgiving, surrendered, obedient heart. She has been very instrumental in bringing these books to pass, as well as strengthening Hearts of Prayer Ministries — may God richly bless and keep you as you faithfully bring your husband, children and all those marriages and hearts we pray for daily to God's throne of grace and mercy.

For every praying wife, mother, grandmother, and faithful servant of Christ who loves the lovable and the unlovable with the heart and power of God in prayer — this book is dedicated to you!

Alphabet Prayers

CONTENTS

INTRODUCTION

It is my prayer that this book of Alphabet Prayers will be the beginning of a beautiful, more intimate, ever-growing personal relationship with our all-loving heavenly Father, God Almighty. Not only for those you pray for, but yourselves as well. Praying Scripture into the lives and hearts of our husbands, children, and pastors is God's highest and holiest calling for every daughter of God, every wife, every mother. Not only are we being sanctified through His Word and Holy Spirit as we pray Scripture — we are sending out His Word and His power into the lives of those we love, empowering them with the power of the Lord! Hosea 1:7 says it is the Lord that saves: *"Yet I will show love to the house of Judah; and I will save them — not by bow, sword or battle, or by horses and horsemen, but by the LORD their God."*

Unfortunately, for so many, prayer is the last thing on the to-do list, or saved as a last resort. So many times we try to change, persuade, and "fix" things on our own — people and situations. This only wreaks havoc, setting up those we love and ourselves for failure and condemnation, rather than success, in all areas of life. Maybe we have dreams of what "we want" our husbands and children to be and do — that may have nothing to do with God's perfect plans for their lives. Searching deeply into our hearts, we may find prayers of our own words and desires to be selfish. Our "flesh" will motivate our prayers to the ends that they and we "look good" to every one else and "feel good" to us. If you struggle and wonder if God is listening, and wonder why He doesn't seem to "be moving" in the lives of your loved ones, take heart! Praying godly virtues, His desires for them in Scripture, will put us right back on the "godly track" and keep us there.

All of us want our husbands and children to be successful in their spiritual, mental, emotional and physical areas. We desire this for our pastors and want to benefit from their preaching, teaching, and ministering to our churches and its members. As loving and caring spouses, mothers, and church members, we desire the very best that God has to offer. Wherever and whatever they do, our highest hopes and prayers for them must be in line with God's will. Whether God calls our families into missionary work abroad or in the neighborhood, schools, or workplace, He has His holy purposes for each of those we pray for, whatever desires He has for them. We must trust Him, and allow them to succeed victoriously, bringing glory to God in His choosing. Prayer must fuel all of this. Scripture prayers are essential for every believer to carry out God's holiest purposes and very best — good pleasing and perfect will for their lives. An intimate daily relationship with and reliance upon the Lord is the only way to achieve God's very best for every believer. God has each and every one of us here for His purpose — to achieve God's plans for our lives, which will be for His Kingdom, and to His glory. Each believer needs Him and He acts in answer to prayer.

We were created as women to be our husband's "helpmates." I've tried many different ways, and the best and only REAL WAY I can help, support, encourage and love my husband is through prayer, prayer for him and prayer that enables me to unconditionally, lovingly be the godly wife and mother God desires me to be. God never ceases to amaze me with His sense of humor. As I was writing this book, adding to my own Scripture prayers, I was "seeking" that perfect family! Well, do you know what I found out? God said, "YOU FIRST!" Many times when our husbands or children are hurting and disobeying, we want to focus on fixing "them" and not the sin. Many times He is pointing out our own flaws and working on them through the actions of those closest to us. Praying God's Word will take them and us where God needs us, to grow and be conformed to the image of His Son. We won't just focus on the "actions" and how they help or hurt us, but the Holy Spirit will help us see how God is calling us to surrender our own hearts to be changed, enabling us to love, forgive, and appropriately support their needs in prayer. Jesus tells us in Mark 12:30-31 that the greatest command is to *"'Love the Lord your God with all your heart and with all your soul and with all your mind and with all your strength.' The second is this: 'Love your neighbor as yourself.' There is no greater commandment than these."* (NIV) These commands cannot be kept without God's power, wrought through and in answer to prayer. Love comes out of and is only possible when fueled by true prayer. Prayer is love, and love prays.

We must be willing to sacrifice sleep, time, and self in every way, entering into God's presence always approaching His throne, finding His grace in our husband's times of need, our children's times of need, and our times of need. No longer will we rely on the telephone, calling to complain or gain another's sympathies — our first response, our daily one, will be getting on our knees and DIALING GOD DAILY. Daily Scripture prayers will keep us from needing to dial "911 Prayers" quite so often. Praying God's Word renews our minds, preparing our hearts that we may be able to test, approve and pray God's will as we pray for those we love (Romans 12:2). Calling upon Him out of pure and obedient hearts we shall be filled with faith and hope, joy and peace. Full of His love and His compassion we will be enabled to joyfully allow God to love our spouses, our children and others through us. Praying for our families, gives great comfort, knowing that God desires the absolute best in each and every situation for each one of His children. He will enable, instruct, conform, transform and persuade each of those we love into His very best, as we pray. It always comforts and fills me with faith as I am praying God's Word for my family, because it reminds me how He loves them even more than I can imagine. Knowing He sent His one and only Son to sacrifice His life on the cross, that He alone is all-powerful, all-knowing, all-seeing, and all-loving; I can with all love and faith bring my family, trusting their hearts totally, into His care, however He chooses to answer my prayers. In who else's hands would we desire our loved one's hearts?

It is God's will for each believer, by God to *"be set apart and holy"* (Leviticus 20:7-8) for Him and for His plans. It is God's will that each of His children be sanctified and crucified to self. (1 Thessalonians 4:3-4). We cannot accomplish these things with our own efforts, our own words, or our own hearts — it must be God's power, for God's purposes, and with Christ's passion. Even Jesus, while here on earth, did not count on His own flesh to accomplish God's purposes and plans for His life. We must not either! Jesus relied upon praying to His heavenly Father, receiving His power and thus being able to carry out His plans (God's will) victoriously!

Jesus spoke Scripture to defeat the devil, to teach his disciples and to love all those God has given Him. He came (the Word made flesh), and left us with His power (the Holy Spirit) and His Word — that is living and active (Hebrews 4:12). Isaiah 55:11 tells us *"so is my word that goes out from my mouth; It will not return to me empty, but will accomplish what I desire and achieve the purpose for which I sent it."* **God's Word does not return to Him void** — it ACCOMPLISHES HIS PURPOSES – **SPEAK IT ALOUD!** God's Word is POWER — our power in life and prayer. When we are praying Scripture, we can be assured we are praying desires that are from God's heart through ours. Prayers that we pray in accordance with His will begin with Him and are sent through our hearts and prayers empowered and led by the Holy Spirit. By praying His Word and desires for those we love, we are agreeing with His Will, and speaking life into the godly virtues He seeks for us, releasing God's blessings to be poured out from heaven.

He also tells us, *"And yet the reason you don't have what you want is that you don't ask God for it."* (James 4:2) How many times do we desire our spouses and children to "do" a certain thing or "behave" a certain way — the way WE WANT and think WE CAN make them do it? I have heard many wives and moms say — no matter how hard "I TRY." Or how many times do we think "if only God would change him/them, my job would be A LOT easier!" Either we ask incorrectly or we keep "doing" instead of praying! Yes, I speak from experience — trying to convince, persuade, and manipulate instead of pray. Not that we should never speak, but I've learned from experience that the quieter and more prayerful I am, the more I stay out of God's way so He can bring forth His blessings faster. God does also instruct us as parents to train our children in the way they should go — but this is useless without prayer. We may hope to "modify" someone's behavior for a short time by making physical reprimands, withholding treats, or offering treats, but only God can mold their hearts to be truly conformed into the godly servants He desires them to be. Remaining in prayer of His Word and virtues, He'll show us when to act, responding appropriately, according to His Word, and when not to respond at all! Remember, our husbands and children are not really "ours," but God's. Our "jobs" are loving them unconditionally, reflecting Christ, and praying His Word into their hearts and lives that HE may conform them and prepare them for how He desires to use them to His glory, in answer to prayer.

Prayer and Scripture are interdependent. Personally, I start my "quiet time" beginning with Scripture prayer, then some daily Bible study, and I end in prayer. Quite frequently I am led back and forth between prayer and Scripture as God speaks to my heart. As you learn to pray Scripture, **always pray in the Holy Spirit,** and be ready for some life-changing transformation of yourself even before those you pray for! Oftentimes I find when I am praying a "verse"/ "virtue" that I think my husband or one of my children "needs" — IT IS *ME* GOD

IS TALKING TO!! I CANNOT PRAY FOR OR TAKE THOSE I PRAY FOR SOMEWHERE I AM NOT, OR AM NOT WILLING TO GO! Just as a teacher cannot teach something he or she doesn't KNOW, neither can a "prayer" pray something he or she doesn't know. When we are praying God's Word into the lives we love, we are not only sending forth His power to sanctify, transform, empower and encourage those we love — *we are first sanctified and transformed* — into the image of His own Son, that *we* may BE EMPOWERED!

May I encourage you as you begin or are continuing to pray Scripture into lives of those you love, keep track of some specific areas of concern as well as praises in the back of this book. Please, do not stop using this book at the end of your thirty-one days; continue each month anew. I believe as you experience God's power and presence in your lives and those you pray for, you won't ever do anything but pray Scripture. Not that you can't and won't cry out to God with your own words at all. But that as you pray Scripture the Holy Spirit will blend all your thoughts and prayers from Scripture, from God's heart. You'll also find that in praying Scripture, you will memorize those verses most meaningful to you without actually trying to do it!

As you get used to praying Scripture and the months go on, start adding some of your own favorite verses that God brings to your heart during Scripture reading time, during a sermon or Sunday school class. If a particular Scripture stands out to you, even if you're not sure why — start praying it!! God is using it to prepare you for His purpose. I've found in the very immediate future. This is one way God will many times speak through the Holy Spirit to your heart — by a verse just "standing out." This is God speaking — LISTEN!!

Praying these Scriptures will help you to watch and listen from and for God's point of view, as His Spirit leads and teaches you how to appropriately pray for *your* husband's needs, as well as your children's and your own. Also, as the Spirit leads and enables, pray for others — add new people you see God bring into the lives of your husband and children, as you remain in daily prayer for them. Really focus on the Scriptures you're praying — meditate upon them throughout out the day, teach them to your children, and memorize them, too. As you put these things into practice you'll put yourself in the mind-set to remain thankful and watchful as you pray, seeing every opportunity, every obstacle, every joy and every tear as an answer to prayer, an opportunity to grow closer to God. It is very exciting, as you pray Scripture, to see God's power at work in the hearts of those you love. And you will be doubly blessed not only to share in their journey of joys and triumphs, but God will heal and bless your heart as you pray HIS WORD as well.

MAY GOD BLESS YOU AND THOSE YOU PRAY FOR
as you follow Paul's exhortation to us in Colossians 4:2 to:

"DEVOTE YOURSELVES TO PRAYER,
BEING WATCHFUL AND THANKFUL."

31 DAYS
of
"ALPHABET PRAYERS"
For Your Husband

*Or again, how can anyone enter a strong man's house
and carry off his possessions
unless he first ties up the strong man?
Then he can rob his house.*

MATTHEW 12:29

May choose one or all three per day of month, as led by the Holy Spirit

DAILY: ASK GOD'S HEDGE OF
PROTECTION & FILLING OF HIS SPIRIT

1. ABIDE:

MATTHEW 11:28-30

Then, as YOU, Jesus said, I pray that --- will come to YOU, he who is weary and carries heavy burdens, and I CLAIM YOUR PROMISE, YOU will give him rest. I pray that he will take YOUR yoke upon him. I pray he will let YOU teach him, because YOU are humble and gentle, and I PRAISE YOU, that then, he will find rest for his soul. For YOUR yoke fits perfectly, and the burden YOU give him is light.

PSALM 91:1, 11 AND 1 JOHN 4:15-17

I pray that --- will live in the shelter of YOU, Most High, and that he will find rest in the shadow of YOU Almighty. For YOU, I PRAISE — order YOUR angels to protect him wherever he goes. YOU PROMISE — all who proclaim that Jesus, the Son of YOU, God, have YOU, God, living in them, and that they live in YOU. And, so I pray that he will know how much YOU love him, and that he will put his trust in YOU. YOU are love, and I pray he will live in love, living in YOU, God, and YOU in him. And as he lives in YOU, I PRAISE YOU, that his love grows more perfect — so he will not be afraid on the day of judgment, but he will face YOU with confidence because he will be like YOU, Christ, in this world.

JOHN 15:5 AND COLOSSIANS 2:6-7

Yes, YOU are the vine; we are the branches. I pray that --- will remain in YOU, and YOU then will remain in him, and YOU PROMISE that he will then produce much fruit. For, I pray that he will know, that apart from YOU, he can do nothing. And now, I pray, just as he accepted YOU, Christ Jesus, as his Lord, I pray that he will continue to live in obedience to YOU. I pray that his roots will grow down deep into YOU and draw up nourishment from YOU, so that he will grow in faith, strong and vigorous in the truth

I pray he is taught. And I pray that his life will overflow with thanksgiving for all that YOU have done.

2. ℬOLD:

HEBREW 4:16

So, I pray that --- will come boldly to YOUR throne - our gracious God. For, there YOU PROMISE, he will receive YOUR mercy, and he will find grace to help him when we need it.

EPHESIANS 6:19-20

And I pray for --- , too. I ask YOU, God, to give him the right words as, I pray, he will boldly explain YOUR secret plan that the Good News is for the Gentiles, too. He, I pray, will be in chains for preaching this message as YOUR ambassador. But I pray that he will always keep on speaking boldly for YOU, as he should.

2 TIMOTHY 1:7 AND JOSHUA 1:9

For YOU, God, have not given --- a spirit of fear and timidity, but I pray he will live by YOUR Spirit of power, love, and self-discipline. And, as YOU have commanded him, I pray that he will be strong and courageous! I pray he will not be afraid or discouraged. For, YOU, Lord, his God PROMISE — YOU are with him wherever he goes.

3. ℭONTENT:

PROVERBS 23:17

I pray that --- will not envy sinners, but always continue to fear YOU, LORD.

PROVERBS 19:23

I pray that --- will grow in his fear of YOU, LORD, that, YOU PROMISE gives him life, security, and protection from harm.

1 TIMOTHY 6:6, 8-10

I pray that --- will have true religion with contentment that is great wealth. So as he has enough food and clothing, I pray he will be content. I pray that he will not long to be rich, falling into temptation and being trapped by many foolish desires that would plunge him into ruin and destruction. I pray that YOU would keep him from the love of money, that is the root to all kinds of evil, and that he would not be like some people who, craving money, have wandered from the faith and pierced themselves with many sorrows.

4. COMMITTED:

PROVERBS 16:3, 8-9

I pray that --- will commit his work to YOU, LORD, and then YOU PROMISE his plans will succeed. It is better for him to be poor and godly than rich and dishonest. He can make his plans, but, I PRAISE YOU, that YOU, LORD, determine his steps.

1 PETER 4:16, 19

However, I pray if --- suffers as a Christian, that he will not be ashamed, but praise YOU, God, that he bears YOUR name. So then, I pray when he suffers according to YOUR will, that he will commit himself to YOU, his faithful Creator, and continue to do good. (NIV)

PSALM 37:5-7A

I pray that --- will commit everything he does to YOU, LORD. I pray he will trust YOU, and YOU PROMISE YOU will help him. YOU will make his innocence as clear as the dawn, and the justice for his cause will shine like the noonday sun. I pray that he will be still in the presence of YOU, LORD, and that he will wait patiently for YOU to act.

5. DEVOTED:

PROVERBS 5:15, 18-19

I pray that --- will always drink water from his own well — I pray he will share his love only with me, his wife. Let me always be a fountain of blessing for him. I pray that he will rejoice in me, the wife of his youth. I pray I will be a loving doe, a graceful deer to him. Let my breasts satisfy him always. May he always be captivated by my love.

1 CORINTHIANS 6:18-20

I pray that --- will run away from sexual sin! No other sin so clearly affects his body as this one does. For sexual immorality is a sin against his own body. I pray he will be convicted and know that his body is the temple of YOUR Holy Spirit, who lives in him and was given to him by YOU, God. He does not belong to himself, for YOU, God, bought him with a high price. So, I pray that he will always honor YOU, God, with his body.

ROMANS 12:9-10

I pray that --- won't just pretend that he loves others. I pray he will really love them. I pray he will hate what is wrong and stand on the side of the good. I pray that we will love each other with genuine affection, and I pray we will always take delight in honoring each other.

6. EVEN-TEMPERED:

PROVERBS 17:27

I pray that --- will be a truly wise person who uses few words; and that he will be a person with understanding that is even-tempered.

1 TIMOTHY 3:2-4

I pray that --- will be as an elder — that he will be a man whose life cannot be spoken against. He, I pray, will be faithful to me, his wife. I pray he will always exhibit self-control, live wisely, and have a good reputation. I pray that he will enjoy having guests in our home and he, I pray, will be able to teach. I pray he will not be a heavy drinker or be violent. He, I pray, will be gentle, peace loving and not one who loves money. He, I pray, will manage our own family well, with our children who respect and obey him.

TITUS 2:2

I pray that --- will be temperate, worthy of respect, self-controlled, and sound in faith, in love and in endurance. (NIV)

7. FAITH:

JOHN 14:12-14

I pray that --- will know, experience, and believe, that YOU have told us: the truth is, that he who believes in YOU will do the same works YOU have done, and I pray that he will do even greater works, because YOU have gone to be with YOUR Father. YOU PROMISE that he can ask for anything in YOUR name and I CLAIM YOUR PROMISE, that YOU will do it, because the work of YOU, the Son, brings glory to YOUR Father. Yes, I pray he will have the faith to ask anything in YOUR name and YOU will do it!

1 TIMOTHY 6:11-12

But, as --- belongs to YOU, God, I pray that he will run from all these evil things, and follow what is right and good. I pray he will pursue a godly life, along with faith, love, perseverance, and gentleness. I pray he will fight the good fight for what he believes. I pray he will hold tightly to the eternal life that YOU, God, have given him, which he has confessed so well before many witnesses.

1 THESSALONIANS 1:3

As I pray for ---, I talk to YOU, God and Father, about him, I think of and I pray that he will complete his faithful work, I pray for his loving deeds and his continual anticipation of the return of YOU, our Lord Jesus Christ.

8. *F*ATHER:

PROVERBS 3:12

For YOU, LORD, correct those YOU love, just as I pray that —will be a father that corrects our children in whom I pray, he delights.

PROVERBS 13:24

I pray that --- won't refuse to discipline our children, as it would prove that he didn't love them; I pray that instead — he will love his children, and I pray that he will always be prompt to discipline them.

PROVERBS 19:18

I pray that --- will discipline our children while there is hope. If he doesn't, he will ruin their lives.

9. *G*ENEROUS:

PROVERBS 22:9

Blessed are those whom — I pray that --- will be generous, because I pray he will feed the poor.

PSALM 112:5-6

I CLAIM YOUR PROMISE, that all goes well for ---, who I pray will be generous, I pray he will lend freely and conduct his business fairly. Such people, YOU PROMISE, then will not be overcome by evil circumstances. I pray he will be righteous that he will be long remembered.

PROVERBS 11:24-25

It is possible to, and I pray that — will give freely and become more wealthy, but I pray he will not be stingy or he would lose everything. I pray he will be the generous one whom YOU prosper and with whom YOU are satisfied; I pray he will refresh others and I CLAIM YOUR PROMISE, that he will himself be refreshed.

10. *H*UMBLE:

PROVERBS 22:1, 3-4

I pray that --- will choose a good reputation over great riches, for being held in high esteem is better than having silver or gold. I pray he will be a prudent person who foresees the danger ahead and takes precautions; I pray he will not be the simpleton who goes blindly on and suffers the consequences. I pray YOU will bless him with true humility and the fear of YOU, LORD, that will lead him to riches, honor and long life.

1 PETER 5:6-7

So, I pray that --- will humble himself under the mighty power of YOU, God, and in YOUR good time — I CLAIM YOUR PROMISE, that YOU will honor him. I pray he will always give all his worries and cares to YOU, God, for I pray he will know that YOU care about what happens to him.

PROVERBS 29:23

I pray for ---. I pray that YOU will cast out all pride that ends in humiliation, and I pray that YOU will bless him with humility that brings him honor.

11. *I*NTEGRITY:

PSALM 25:21

May integrity and honesty protect ---, for I pray that he will put his hope in you.

PROVERBS 10:8-9

I pray that --- will be wise and glad to be instructed, but I pray he will not be a babbling fool who falls flat on his face. I pray he will be a person with integrity that YOU PROMISE has firm footing, but I pray he will not be one who follows crooked paths, and will slip and fall.

PROVERBS 13:6

I pray for ---, pour out YOUR SPIRIT of righteousness that YOU PROMISE —guards the man of integrity — that I pray he will always be, and then I PRAISE YOU, that he will not be touched by the wickedness that overthrows the sinner.

12. *J*OY / PEACE:

PROVERBS 29:15, 17

I pray that --- will lovingly discipline and reprimand our children that YOU PROMISE — produces wisdom. I pray I will not be a mother who would be disgraced by undisciplined children. I pray he will discipline our children, and I PRAISE YOU, that then they will give us happiness and peace of mind.

PROVERBS 15:30

I pray that YOU will bless --- with a cheerful look that brings joy to his heart; and I pray YOU will bless him with good news that makes for his good health.

PSALM 28:7

I pray that YOU alone, O, LORD, are ---'s strength, his shield from every danger. I pray he will trust in YOU with all his heart. I CLAIM YOUR PROMISE TO then help him, and I PRAISE YOU, that his heart will be filled with joy. I THANK YOU that he will then burst out in songs of thanksgiving.

13. $\mathscr{K}$NOWLEDGE/ FEAR LORD:

PSALM 128:1-4, 6

How I pray --- will be happy as I pray that he fears YOU, LORD —
he whom I pray will always follow YOUR ways! He, then — I
CLAIM YOUR PROMISE — will enjoy the fruit of his labor. How
happy, I pray, he will be! How rich his life! I, his wife, will be like
a fruitful vine, flourishing within our home. And look at all those
children! There they sit around our table as vigorous and healthy as
young olive trees. That is YOUR reward, for he, who I pray will fear
YOU. May he live to enjoy our grandchildren. And may he have
quietness and peace.

PROVERBS 3:7-8

I pray that --- will not be impressed with his own wisdom. Instead, I
pray he will fear YOU, LORD, and turn his back on evil. Then I CLAIM
YOUR PROMISE — that he will gain renewed health and vitality.

PROVERBS 14:26-27

I pray that --- will fear YOU, LORD and YOU PROMISE, he will be
secure; I PRAISE YOU, that YOU will be a place of refuge for our
children. I pray YOU will bless him with the fear of YOU, LORD, that
is a life-giving fountain; it offers him escape from the snares of death.

14. $\mathscr{L}$OOSED STRONGHOLDS:

2 CORINTHIANS 10:4-6

I pray that --- will use YOUR mighty weapons, not mere worldly
weapons, to knock down the devil's strongholds. With these
weapons I PRAISE YOU, that he will break down every proud argu-
ment that keeps him from knowing YOU, God. With these
weapons, I pray that he will conquer his rebellious ideas, and he will
teach them to obey YOU, Christ.

EPHESIANS 4:26-17

And I pray that --- will not sin by letting anger gain control over him. I pray he will not let the sun go down while he is still angry, for anger gives a mighty foothold to the devil.

ISAIAH 58:6, 8-9

Is not this the kind of fasting I have chosen? I pray and fast before YOU, Lord, for ---. I pray YOU will loose his chains of injustice and untie the cords of his yoke, I pray that YOU will set him who is oppressed free and break every yoke from him. I CLAIM YOUR PROMISE, that then his light will break forth like the dawn, and his healing will quickly appear; then YOUR righteousness will go before him, and YOUR glory of the Lord will be his rear guard. Then I pray that he will call, and YOU, I PRAISE, Lord, will answer; he, I pray, will cry for help, and YOU will say: Here am I.

15. *L*OVE:

MARK 12:30-31

I pray that --- will love YOU, Lord, his God, with all his heart, all his soul, all his mind, and all his strength. The second is equally important; I pray he will love his neighbor as himself. YOU tell us that no other commandment is greater that these.

COLOSSIANS 3:19, 21

I pray that ---, my husband, will love me, his wife, and never treat me harshly. If he does, I would become discouraged and quit trying.

1 CORINTHIANS 13:4-7

I pray YOU will bless --- with love that is patient, love that is kind. I pray YOU will bless him with love — it does not envy, it does not boast, it is not proud. It is not rude, it is not self-seeking, it is not easily angered, and it keeps no record of wrongs. I pray he will be filled with love that does not delight in evil but rejoices with the truth. It always protects, always trusts, always hopes, and always perseveres. (NIV)

16. *M*ERCY/ COMPASSION:

PSALM 103:13

I pray that --- will be like YOU, LORD, are like a father to YOUR children. I pray he also will be tender and compassionate, as YOU are to those who fear YOU.

MATTHEW 5:6-7

YOU PROMISE that YOU bless those who, I pray, --- will be hungry and thirsty for justice for; then he will receive it in full. YOU bless those who, I pray, he will also be merciful, for I CLAIM YOUR PROMISE, that he will be shown mercy.

COLOSSIANS 3:12-13

Since YOU, God, have chosen --- to be among the holy people whom YOU love, I pray he will clothe himself with tenderhearted mercy, kindness, humility, gentleness, and patience. I pray he will make allowance for each other's faults and forgive the person who offends him. I pray he will remember YOU, Lord, forgave him, so he must forgive others.

17. *N*OBLE CHARACTER:

ISAIAH 32:8

I pray that --- will be a good person that he, I pray, will be generous to others and I CLAIM YOUR PROMISE, that he will be blessed for all he does.

PHILIPPIANS 4:8-9

And now, dear brothers and sisters, let me say one more thing as I close this letter. I pray that --- will fix his thoughts on what is true and honorable and right. I pray he will think about things that are pure and lovely and admirable. I pray he will think about things that are excellent and worthy of praise, and I pray he will keep putting into practice all he has learned from YOU and heard from YOU and saw YOU doing, and I CLAIM YOUR PROMISE, that YOU, God of peace, will be with him.

2 TIMOTHY 2:21-22

I pray that --- will keep himself pure, that he will be a utensil that YOU, God, can use for YOUR purpose. I pray his life will be clean, and that he will be ready for YOU, his Master, to use him for every good work. I pray he will always run from anything that stimulates youthful lust. I pray he will follow anything that makes him want to do right. I pray he will pursue faith and love and peace, and enjoy the companionship of those who call on YOU, Lord, with pure hearts.

18. OBEDIENT:

PSALM 103:17-18

I CLAIM YOUR PROMISE that the love of YOU, LORD, remains forever with ---, who I pray will always fear YOU. I PRAISE YOU that YOUR salvation extends to our children's children of him who I pray is faithful to YOUR covenant, of him, who I pray will obey YOUR commandments! And, I pray that he will have a clear conscience, that he can come to YOU with bold confidence. I PRAISE YOU, that he will receive whatever he requests from YOU, because — I pray that he obeys YOU and does the things that please YOU. And this is YOUR commandment: I pray that he will believe in the name of YOUR Son, Jesus Christ, and that he will love one another, just as YOU have commanded us. YOU PROMISE, that he who obeys YOUR commandments lives in fellowship with YOU, and YOU with him. And we know that YOU live in him because I PRAISE YOU, that YOUR Holy Spirit lives in him.

DEUTERONOMY 30:2, 5-10

I pray that --- will always return to YOU, LORD our God, and I pray he and our children will wholeheartedly obey all YOUR commands YOU have given him today. Then, I CLAIM YOUR PROMISE, YOU will return us to the land that belonged to his ancestors, and he will possess that land again. I CLAIM YOUR PROMISE, YOU will make him even more prosperous and numerous than his ancestors! YOU, LORD our God, will cleanse his heart and the hearts of all our descendants so that he and they will love YOU with all their heart and soul, and so they may live! YOU, LORD our God, will inflict all these curses on his enemies and persecutors. Then he will again obey YOU, LORD, and keep all YOUR commands YOU are giving him today. I CLAIM YOUR PROMISE — that, YOU, LORD our God, will make him successful in everything he does. YOU will give him many children and numerous livestock, and his fields will produce abundant harvest, for YOU, LORD, will delight in being good to him as YOU were to his ancestors. YOU, LORD our God, will delight in him as, I pray he will obey YOUR voice and keep YOUR commands and laws that are written in YOUR Book of the Law, and as he, I pray, will turn to YOU, LORD our God, with all his heart and soul.

DEUTERONOMY 6:1-6

I pray that --- will be taught and obey all the commands, laws, and regulations of YOU, LORD our God, in the land he is about to enter and occupy, so he and our children and grandchildren might fear YOU, LORD our God, as long as they live. I pray he will obey all YOUR laws and commands, that he will enjoy a long life. I pray that he will listen closely, to everything YOU say and I pray that he will be careful to obey. Then, I CLAIM YOUR PROMISE that all will go well with him, and he will have many children in the land flowing with milk and honey, just as YOU, LORD, the God of our ancestors, promised him. I pray he will Hear, O, Israel! YOU, LORD are his God, YOU, LORD, alone. And he, I pray, will love YOU, LORD, his God, with all his heart, all his soul, and all his strength. And I pray that he will commit himself wholeheartedly to these commands YOU are giving him today.

19. *P*ERSERVERANCE:

HEBREWS 2:1-2A

Therefore, since --- is surrounded by such a huge crowd of witnesses to his life of faith, I pray he will strip off every weight that slows him down, especially the sin that so easily hinders his progress. And I pray he will run with endurance the race that YOU, God, have set before him. I pray he will do this by keeping his eyes on YOU, Jesus, on whom his faith depends from start to finish. YOU were willing to die a shameful death on the cross because of the joy YOU knew would be YOURS afterward. Now, I PRAISE YOU, as YOU are seated in the place of highest honor beside God's throne in heaven.

2 THESSALONIANS 3:3, 5 AND JUDE 20-21, 24

But YOU, Lord, are faithful; YOU, I pray for ---, will make him strong and guard him from the evil one. May YOU, Lord, bring him into an even deeper understanding of the love of YOU, God, and the endurance that comes from YOU, Christ. And I pray that he will continue to build his life on the foundation of his most holy faith, and that he will continue to pray as he is directed by YOUR Holy Spirit. I pray that he will live in such a way that YOUR love can bless him as he waits for the eternal life that YOU, our Lord Jesus Christ, in YOUR mercy is going to give him. And now, all glory to YOU, who is able to keep him from stumbling, and who will bring him into YOUR glorious presence innocent of sin and with great joy.

2 PETER 1:5-8

So I pray that --- will make every effort to apply the benefits of these — YOUR promises to his life. Then I pray his faith will produce a life of moral excellence. I pray YOU will bless him with a life of moral excellence that leads to knowing YOU, God, better. Knowing YOU, God, leads to his self-control. Self-control leads to his godliness. Godliness leads to his love for other Christians, and finally I pray he will grow to have genuine love for everyone. The more he grows like this, the more, YOU PROMISE, he will become productive and useful in his knowledge of YOU, our Lord Jesus Christ.

20. PROVIDER:

PROVERBS 3:9-10

I pray that --- will honor YOU, LORD, with his wealth and with the best part of everything his land produces. Then, I CLAIM YOUR PROMISE, YOU will fill his barns with grain, and his vats will overflow with the finest wine.

TITUS 3:14

I pray that --- will not have an unproductive life. I pray he will learn to do good by helping others who have urgent needs.

PSALM 1:1-3

Oh, I pray that --- will inherit the joys of those who will not follow the advice of the wicked, or stand around with sinners, or join in with scoffers. But, I pray that he will delight in doing everything YOU, his LORD, wants; day and night — I pray he will think about YOUR law. Then, YOU PROMISE, he will be like trees planted along the riverbank; he will be bear fruit each season without fail. His leaves will never wither, and in all he does, he will prosper.

21. QUIET / PRAYERFUL:

PSALM 131:1-3

LORD, I pray that ---'s heart is not proud; and his eyes are not haughty. I pray that he will not concern himself with matters too great or awesome for him. But, I pray that he will still and quiet himself, just as a small child is quiet with its mother. Yes, like a small child, I pray his soul is within him. O, I pray he will put his hope in YOU, LORD — now and always.

PSALM 32:6-8

Therefore, I pray that --- will, along with all the godly, confess his rebellion to YOU while there is time, that he may not drown in the floodwaters of judgment. For YOU, I pray, are his hiding place; then YOU protect him from trouble. I PRAISE YOU, that then — YOU will surround him with songs of victory. I CLAIM YOUR PROMISE, YOU, LORD, say, "YOU will guide him along the best pathway for his life."

PHILIPPIANS 4:6-7

I pray that --- will not worry about anything, instead, that he will pray about everything. I pray he will always tell YOU, God, what he needs, and thank YOU for all that YOU have done. As he does this, I CLAIM YOUR PROMISE that he will experience YOUR peace, which is far more wonderful than the human mind can understand. I THANK YOU, that YOUR peace will guard his heart and mind as, I pray, he will live in YOU, Christ Jesus.

22. REPENTANT:

PSALM 32:1-2

Oh, what joy for --- whose rebellion is forgiven, I pray YOU will keep him repentant, whose sin is put out of sight! Yes, what joy for him whose record YOU, Lord, have cleared of sin. I pray that his life will always be lived in complete honesty!

1 JOHN 1:7-8

I pray that --- will live in the light of YOUR presence, just as Christ is, then I PRAISE YOU, that he will have fellowship with each other, and the blood of Jesus, YOUR Son, cleanses him from every sin. I pray that he will not say he has no sin; he then would be only fooling himself and I pray he will not ever refuse to accept the truth.

JAMES 5:16, 19

I pray that --- and I will confess our sins to each other and pray for each other so that we may be healed. I PRAISE YOU, that the earnest prayers of he and I, righteous persons, have great power and wonderful results. I pray that if he ever wanders away from the truth — that he would be brought back again. I THANK YOU, that I can be sure that the one who brings him back will save him from death and bring about the forgiveness of many sins.

23. SPIRIT/ SELF-CONTROLLED:

ROMANS 8:13-15

I pray that --- will not follow evil — for if he were to keep on following it, he would perish. But, I pray that he will, through the power of YOUR Holy Spirit, turn from sin and its evil deeds, and YOU PROMISE, that he will live. For he will be led by YOUR Spirit because he, is a child of YOU, God. So I pray he will not be like cowering, fearful slaves. I pray he will behave instead like YOUR very own child, adopted into YOUR family— calling YOU "Father, dear Father."

EPHESIANS 4:30-32

And I pray that --- will not bring sorrow to YOUR Holy Spirit by the way he lives. I pray he will remember that YOU are the one who has identified him as YOUR own, guaranteeing that he will be saved on the day of redemption. I pray that he will get rid of all bitterness, rage, anger, harsh words, and slander, as well as all types of malicious behavior. Instead, I pray he will be kind to others, tenderhearted, and forgiving, just as I PRAISE YOU, God, through Christ, has forgiven him.

1 PETER 5:8-9

I pray that --- will be careful! I pray he will watch out for attacks from the devil, his great enemy. He prowls around like a roaring lion, looking for some victim to devour. I pray he will take a firm stand again him, and be strong in his faith. I pray he will know and remember that his Christian brothers and sisters all over the world are going through the same kind of suffering he is.

24. TRUST:

PSALM 62:5-8

I pray that --- will wait quietly before YOU, God, for I pray his hope is in YOU. YOU, are his rock and his salvation, his fortress where he will not be shaken. I PRAISE YOU, that his salvation and his honor come from YOU, God, alone. I pray he will come to YOU, for YOU are his refuge, a rock where no enemy can reach him. O, Lord, I pray he will trust in YOU at all times. I pray he will pour out his heart to YOU, for YOU, God, are his refuge.

PROVERBS 29:25 AND JEREMIAH 29:11-13

I pray that --- will not fear people, for it is a dangerous trap, but I pray that he will trust YOU, LORD, for YOU PROMISE, that means his safety. I pray he will know that: YOU know the plans YOU have for him, declares YOU, LORD. They are plans for good and not for disaster, to give him a future and a hope. I PRAISE YOU, that when he prays YOU will listen. I pray that he will seek

YOU in earnest, for YOU PROMISE, he will find YOU when he seeks YOU.

PSALM 37:3-4

I pray that --- will trust in YOU, LORD, and do good. Then, I CLAIM YOUR PROMISE, he will live safely in the land and prosper. I pray he will take delight in YOU, LORD, and I CLAIM YOUR PROMISE, that YOU will give him his heart's desires.

25. *T*RAIN / TEACH :

DEUTERONOMY 6:6-9; 11:21

And I pray that --- will commit himself wholeheartedly to these commands YOU are giving him today. I pray that he will repeat them again and again to our children. I pray that he will talk about them when he is at home and when he is away on a journey, when he is lying down and when he is getting up again. I pray he will tie them to his hands as a reminder, and wear them on his forehead. I pray he will write them on the doorposts of our house and on our gates. So that as long as the sky remains above the earth, he and our children may flourish in the land YOU, LORD, swore to give his ancestors.

PROVERBS 22:6, 15

I pray that --- will teach our children to choose the right path, and when they are older, I CLAIM YOUR PROMISE AND PRAISE YOU, that they will remain upon it. A youngster's heart is filled with foolishness, but discipline will drive it away.

EPHESIANS 6:4

And now a word to you fathers. I pray that --- will not make our children angry by the way he treats them. Rather, I pray he will bring them up with the discipline and instruction approved by YOU, Lord.

26. Upright:

PROVERBS 21:21

I pray that --- will pursue godliness and unfailing love and I CLAIM YOUR PROMISE, that he will find life, godliness, and honor.

PSALM 112:1-2

I pray that --- will always praise YOU, Lord! Happy is he, who, I pray, will fear YOU, Lord. Yes, happy will he be, as he delights in doing what YOU command. I CLAIM YOUR PROMISE, then his children will be successful everywhere; his entire generation of godly people will be blessed.

TITUS 2:11-12

For I pray that --- will personally know the grace of YOU, God, which has been revealed, bringing salvation to him and all people. As we are instructed — I pray that he will turn from godless living and sinful pleasures. Instead, I pray that he will live in this evil world with self-control, right conduct, and devotions to YOU, God.

27. Victory/ SANCTIFICATION:

PROVERBS 2:1-8

I pray that --- will listen to YOU and treasure YOUR instructions. I pray he will tune his ears to wisdom, and concentrate on understanding. I pray he will cry out for insight and understanding. I pray he will search for them as he would for lost money or hidden treasure. Then, YOU PROMISE, he will understand what it means to fear YOU, Lord, and he will gain knowledge of YOU, God. For YOU, Lord, will grant him wisdom! From YOUR mouth comes — please bless him with YOUR knowledge and understanding. YOU grant a treasure of good sense to he who is holy. YOU are his shield, protecting him, who I pray will walk with integrity. YOU guard the paths of justice and protect him who I pray will be faithful to YOU.

1 THESSALONIANS 5:23-24

Now may YOU, God of peace, make --- holy in every way, and may his whole spirit and soul and body be kept blameless until that day when YOU, our Lord Jesus Christ, comes again. I PRAISE YOU, that YOU, God, who calls him, is faithful; and I CLAIM YOUR PROMISE, YOU will do this.

1 CORINTHIANS 15:57-58

I pray that --- will always thank YOU, God, who gives him victory over sin and death through YOU, Jesus Christ our Lord! So, I pray that he will be strong and steady, always enthusiastic about YOUR work, for I pray he will know that nothing he does for YOU, Lord, is ever useless.

28. WISE COUNSEL:

PROVERBS 12:5, 26

I PRAISE YOU, that the plans of ---, who is godly, are just; I pray that he will always avoid the advice of the wicked that is treacherous. I pray that he will seek the godly that give good advice to their friends — I pray YOU will bless him with godly friends, and I pray he will avoid the wicked that would lead him astray.

PROVERBS 13:14, 20

I pray that --- will get the advice of the wise that is like a life-giving fountain; I pray that he will accept it, and then he will avoid the snares of death. I pray he will also walk with the wise and I THANK YOU, that he will become wise; I pray he will not walk with fools as he would suffer harm.

PROVERBS 27:6, 17

I pray that --- will receive wounds from a friend that are better than many kisses from an enemy. As iron sharpens iron, I pray he will have a friend that sharpens him, who I pray will also be a friend.

29. *W*OUNDS:

JEREMIAH 33:6, 8

Nevertheless, the time will come when, I PRAISE YOU, that YOU, I pray, will heal ---'s damage and give him prosperity and peace. YOU, I pray, will cleanse away his sins against YOU, and I THANK YOU, that YOU will forgive all his sins of rebellion.

PSALM 147:3

I CLAIM YOUR PROMISE, that YOU heal ---, who is brokenhearted, and I PRAISE YOU, as I pray that YOU will bind up his wounds.

1 PETER 2:24

YOU personally carried away ---'s sins in YOUR own body on the cross so that, I PRAISE YOU — he can be dead to sin and I pray that he will live for what is right. I CLAIM YOUR PROMISE, that he has been healed by YOUR wounds!

30. *Y*OUR WORD:

PROVERBS 4:20-27

I pray that --- will pay attention, for he is YOUR child, to what YOU say. I pray he will listen carefully. I pray he will not lose sight of YOUR words. I pray he will let them penetrate deep within his heart, for they bring life and radiate health to him, who, I pray will discover their meaning. Above all else, I pray that he will guard his heart, for it affects everything he does. I pray he will avoid all perverse talk; and stay far from corrupt speech. I pray he will look straight ahead, and fix his eyes on what lies before him. I pray he will mark out a straight path for his feet; then stick to the path and stay safe. I pray he will not get sidetracked; and that he will keep his feet from following evil.

1 JOHN 5:3-4 AND JEREMIAH 1:7-9

I pray --- will love YOU, God, which means keeping YOUR commandments, and really, that isn't difficult. And I PRAISE YOU, that he, and every child of YOU, God, will defeat this evil world by trusting YOU, Christ, to give him victory. And I pray that he will go wherever YOU send him, and that he will say whatever YOU tell him. I pray that he won't be afraid of the people, for YOU promise to be with him and take care of him. YOU, the LORD, have spoken! I pray that YOU, LORD, will touch his mouth and say that YOU, have put YOUR words into his mouth!

PROVERBS 7:1-5

I pray that --- will follow YOUR advice; he is YOUR son. I pray he will always treasure YOUR commands. I pray he will obey them and live! I pray he will guard YOUR teaching as his most precious possession. I pray that he will tie them on his fingers as a reminder. I pray he will write them deep within his heart. I pray that he will love wisdom like a sister; and make insight a beloved member of his family. I pray he will let them hold him back from an affair with an immoral woman, from listening to the flattery of an adulterous woman.

31. *J*EALOUS/ PASSION LORD:

ROMANS 12:11-13

I pray that --- will never be lazy in his work, but serve YOU, Lord, enthusiastically. I pray he will be glad for all YOU, God, are planning for him. I pray he will be patient in trouble, and always be prayerful. When YOUR children are in need, I pray he will be the one to help them out. And I pray he will get into the habit of inviting guests home for dinner or, if they need lodging, for the night.

PROVERBS 23:17-18

I pray that --- will not envy sinners, but always continue to fear YOU, LORD. For surely he has a future ahead of him; and, I CLAIM YOUR PROMISE, that his hope will not be disappointed.

HEBREWS 10:22-25

I pray that --- will always go right into the presence of YOU God, with a true heart fully trusting YOU. For I PRAISE YOU, that his evil conscience has been sprinkled with Christ's blood to make him clean, and his body has been washed with YOUR pure water. Without wavering, I pray he will hold tightly to the hope he says he has, for YOU, God, can be trusted to keep YOUR promise. I pray also that he will think of ways to encourage one another to outbursts of a love and good deeds. And I pray he will not neglect his meeting together, as some people do, but I pray he will encourage and warn each other, especially now that the day of YOUR coming back again is drawing near.

31 DAYS
of
"ALPHABET PRAYERS"
For Your Children

He said to them, "Let the little children come to me,
And do not hinder them,
For the kingdom of God belongs to such as these."
And he took the children in his arms,
Put his hands on them and blessed them.

MARK 10:14B, 16

May choose one or all three per day of month, as led by the Holy Spirit

(also grandchildren, other special children
God brings into your life)

DAILY: ASK GOD'S HEDGE OF
PROTECTION & FILLING OF HIS SPIRIT

1. $\mathscr{A}$BIDE IN CHRIST

JOHN 15:4, 9-10

I pray that --- will remain in YOU, and YOU will remain in him/her. For no branch can bear good fruit by itself; therefore, I pray that he/she will remain in YOU, the vine. Neither can he/she bear fruit unless he/she remains in YOU. As YOUR Father has loved YOU, JESUS, so have YOU, JESUS, loved him/her. I pray that he/she will obey YOUR commands, I pray he/she will remain in YOUR love, just as YOU have obeyed YOUR Father's commands and remain in his love. (NIV)

1 JOHN 2:5

I pray that --- will obey YOUR word, and I PRAISE YOU, that YOUR love will be truly made complete in him/her. This is how he/she knows he/she is in YOU: I pray as he/she claims to live in YOU, that he/she will walk as YOU did. (NIV)

1 JOHN 3:23-24

And this is YOUR command: I pray --- will believe in the name of YOUR Son, Jesus Christ, and I pray he/she will love one another as YOU have commanded him/her. I pray that he/she obeys YOUR commands and he/she will live in YOU, and YOU in him/her. And this is how he/she knows that YOU live in him/her — he/she knows by YOUR Spirit that YOU gave him/her. (NIV)

2. $\mathscr{A}$CCEPT SALVATION:

ISAIAH 45:8

I pray for ---, that YOU will open up, Oh, Heavens, and pour out YOUR righteousness upon him/her. Let the earth open wide so YOUR salvation and righteousness can sprout up together in him/her. I PRAISE YOU, that YOU, LORD, have created him/her.

PHILIPPIANS 2:12-13

I pray that --- will always be so careful to follow YOUR instructions as when I am/was with him/her. And when I am away I pray he/she will be even more careful to put into action YOUR saving work in his/her life, I pray he/she will be obeying YOU, God, with deep reverence and fear. For YOU, God, I pray will be working in him/her, giving him/her the desire to obey YOU and the power to do what pleases YOU.

2 CORINTHIANS 7:9-10

Now I am glad YOU sent it, not because it hurt ---, but because the pain — I pray will cause him/her to have remorse and change his/her ways. I pray he/she will always have the kind of sorrow that YOU, God, want YOUR people to have. For YOU, God, I ask and CLAIM YOUR PROMISE to use sorrow in his/her life to help him/her turn away from sin and seek YOUR salvation. We will never regret that kind of sorrow. But, I pray he/she will not ever have sorrow without repentance that is the kind that results in death.

3. *B*IBLICAL SELF-WORTH:

PSALM 127:3

I pray that --- will know that he/she is a gift from YOU, LORD; I pray he/she will know he/she is a reward from YOU.

EPHESIANS 2:10

For I pray that --- will know he/she is YOUR masterpiece. That YOU have created him/her anew in YOU, Christ Jesus, so that he/she can, and I pray that he/she will do the good things YOU planned for him/her long ago.

EPHESIANS 4:23-24

I pray that there will be a spiritual renewal of ---'s thoughts and attitudes. I pray he/she will display a new nature because he/she is a new person, created in YOUR likeness —righteous, holy, and true.

4. *C*OURAGEOUS:

DEUTERONOMY 31:6

I pray --- will be strong and courageous! I pray he/she will not be afraid of them! YOU, LORD, his/her God, will go ahead of him/her. I PRAISE YOU, that YOU will neither fail him/her nor forsake him/her.

JOSHUA 1:7-9

I pray --- will obey YOUR command to be strong and very courageous. I pray he/she will obey all the laws Moses gave him/her. I pray he/she will not turn away from them, and I CLAIM YOUR PROMISE, that he/she will be successful in everything he/she does. I pray he/she will study this book of YOUR Law, being sure to obey all that is written in it. Only then will he/she succeed. YOU command him/her — and I pray that he/she will be strong and courageous! I pray he/she will not be afraid or discouraged. For YOU PROMISE, YOU, LORD, his/her God, is with him/her wherever he/she goes.

EPHESIANS 6:10, 19

A final word: I pray that --- will be strong with YOUR mighty power. And I pray for him/her, too. I ask YOU, God, to give him/her the right words as I pray he/she will boldly explain YOUR secret plan that the Good News of YOUR Salvation is for the Gentiles, too.

5. *C*ONTENT:

PROVERBS 19:23

I pray that YOU will bless --- with the fear of YOU, LORD, for YOU PROMISE it leads him/her to life: Then I PRAISE YOU, that he/she will be one that rests content, untouched by trouble. (NIV)

PHILIPPIANS 4:10-14

How grateful I pray that --- will always be, and how I pray he/she will praise YOU, Lord, that others, I pray will be concerned about him/her again. I pray he/she will always know others have always been concerned for him/her, but for a while they didn't have the chance to help him/her. Not that I pray he/she will not ever be in need, for I pray he/she will learn how to get along happily whether he/she has much or little. I pray he/she will know how to live on almost nothing or with everything. I pray he/she will learn the secret of living in every situation, whether it is with a full stomach or empty, with plenty or little. For I CLAIM YOUR PROMISE, that he/she can do everything with the help of YOU, Christ, who gives him/her the strength he/she needs. But even so, I PRAY YOU will send someone to share with him/her in his/her present difficulty.

HEBREWS 13:4-5

I pray that --- will always give honor to marriage, and remain faithful to one another in marriage. YOU, God, will surely judge people, and I pray he/she will not be one of those who are immoral and those who commit adultery. I pray he/she will stay away from the love of money, and always be satisfied with what he/she has. For YOU, God, have said, I PRAISE YOU, that YOU will never fail him/her. YOU will never forsake him/her.

6. *D*EVOTED:

1 CHRONICLES 22:19A AND PSALM 37:5

Now, I pray that --- will seek YOU, LORD our God, with all his/her heart. I pray that he/she will commit everything he/she does to YOU, LORD. I pray that he/she will trust YOU, and YOU PROMISE YOU will help him/her.

PSALM 86: 2-7

I pray that YOU will protect --- for I pray he/she will be devoted to YOU. I pray YOU will save him/her, for I pray he/she will serve YOU and trust YOU. YOU are his/her God. Be merciful, O, LORD for I pray that he/she will be calling on YOU constantly. I pray that YOU will give him/her happiness O, LORD, for his/her life depends on YOU. O, LORD, YOU are so good, so ready to forgive, so full of unfailing love for him/her, who I pray will ask YOUR aid. Listen closely to his/her prayer. O, LORD; hear his/her urgent cries. I pray he/she will call to YOU whenever trouble strikes and YOU PROMISE, that YOU will answer him/her.

COLOSSIANS 4:2, 5

I pray that --- will always devote himself/herself to prayer, being watchful and thankful. I pray that he/she will live wisely among those who are not Christians, and that he/she will make the most of every opportunity. I pray, too, that his/her conversation will be gracious and effective so that he/she will have the right answer for everyone.

7. ENDURANCE:

2 CORINTHIANS 6:4-10

I pray for ---, that in everything he/she does that he/she will try to show that he/she is a true minister of YOU, God. I pray he/she will patiently endure troubles and hardships and calamities of every kind. Even if he/she is beaten, put in jail, or faces angry mobs, is worked to exhaustion, endures sleepless nights, and goes without food. I pray that he/she will prove himself/herself by his/her purity, his/her understanding, his/her patience, his/her kindness, his/her sincere love, and the power of YOUR Holy Spirit. I pray he/she will faithfully preach YOUR truth. YOUR power, I pray, will work in him/her. I pray he/she will have righteousness as his/her weapon, both to attack and to defend himself/herself. I pray he/she will serve YOU, God, whether people honor him/her or despise him/her, whether they slander him/her or praise him/her. I pray he/she will always be honest, even if others call him/her impostors. We are well known, but we are treated as unknown. We live close to death, but here we are, still alive. We have been beaten within an inch of our lives. Our hearts ache, but I pray he/she will always have joy. We are poor, but I pray he/she will always give spiritual riches to others. We own nothing, and yet I CLAIM YOUR PROMISE, he/she will have everything.

2 THESSALONIANS 3:3, 5

But YOU, Lord, are faithful; YOU, I pray, will make --- strong and guard him/her from the evil one. May YOU, Lord, bring him/her into an even deeper understanding of the love of YOU, God and the endurance that comes from YOU, Christ.

COLOSSIANS 4:17

And I pray that --- will be sure to carry out the work that YOU, Lord, give him/her.

8. FRIENDS:

PROVERBS 1:8-10, 15-16

I pray that --- will listen, my child — to what his/her father teaches him/her. I pray he/she will not neglect my teaching. I pray he/she will learn from them, YOU PROMISE, they will crown him/her with grace and clothe him/her with honor. My child, if sinners entice him/her, I pray he/she will turn his/her back on them. I pray he/she will not go along with them, my child! I pray he/she will stay far away from their paths. They rush to commit crimes. They hurry to commit murder.

PSALM 1:1-3

Oh, I pray that YOU will bless --- with the joys of those who do not follow the advice of the wicked, or stand around with sinners, or join in with scoffers. But, instead, I pray he/she will delight in doing everything that YOU, Lord, want; day and night I pray he/she will always think about YOUR law. Then, YOU PROMISE, he/she will be like trees planted along the riverbank, bearing his/her fruit each season without fail. His/her leaves never wither, and in all he/she does, I PRAISE YOU, that, he/she will prosper.

2 CORINTHIANS 6:14, 16-18

I pray that --- will not team up with those who are unbelievers. How can goodness be a partner with wickedness? How can light live with darkness? And what union can there be between him/her, YOUR temple and idols? For I pray that he/she will know, he/she is the temple of YOU, our living God. As YOU, God, said: YOU will live in him/her and walk among him/her. YOU, I pray will be his/her God, and he/she will be YOUR people. Therefore, I pray he/she will come out from them and separate himself/herself from them, says YOU, Lord. I pray he/she will not touch their filthy things, and I CLAIM YOUR PROMISE, that YOU will welcome him/her. And YOU will be his/her Father, and he/she will be YOUR sons and daughters, says YOU, Lord Almighty.

9. FAITH:

1 THESSALONIANS 1:3-6

As I talk to YOU, God and Father, about ---, I think of and pray he/she will complete and be commended for his/her faithful work, his/her loving deeds, and his/her continual anticipation of the return of YOU, his/her Lord Jesus Christ. I pray he/she will know that YOU, God, love him/her, and that YOU have chosen him/her to be YOUR own people. For I pray when he/she is brought the Good News, it is not only with words but I pray it will come to him/her also with YOUR power, for YOUR Holy Spirit, I pray, will give him/her full assurance that what we say is true. And I pray he/she will know that the way my husband and I live among him/her will be further proof of the truth of YOUR message. So, I pray that he/she will receive YOUR message with joy from YOUR Holy Spirit in spite of the severe suffering it brought him/her. In this way, I pray he/she will imitate YOU, Lord and us.

1 TIMOTHY 6:11-12

Since --- belongs to YOU, God, I pray he/she will run from all these evil things, and follow what is right and good. I pray he/she will pursue a godly life, along with faith, love, perseverance, and gentleness. I pray he/she will fight the good fight for what he/she believes. I pray he/she will hold tightly to the eternal life that YOU, God, has given him/her, which he/she, I pray, will confess so well before many witnesses.

HEBREWS 11:1, 6

What is faith? I pray that YOU will bless --- with abundant, increasing faith and I pray he/she will be filled with the confident assurance that what he/she hopes for is going to happen. I pray that YOU will fill him/her with the evidence of things he/she cannot yet see. So, I pray he/she will see it is impossible to please YOU, God, without faith. I pray he/she will always want to come to YOU, and that he/she will believe that there is YOU, God, and that YOU reward him/her who, I pray, will sincerely seek YOU.

10. *G*ENTLE/ KINDNESS:

GALATIANS 5:16, 22-26

So I pray that --- will live according to his/her new life in YOUR Holy Spirit. And I pray he/she won't be doing what his/her sinful nature craves. I PRAISE YOU, that when YOUR Holy Spirit controls his/her life, YOU will produce this kind of fruit in him/her: love, joy, peace, patience, kindness, goodness, faithfulness, gentleness, and self-control. Here there is no conflict with the law. I pray, as he/she belongs to YOU, Christ Jesus, he/she will nail the passions and desires of his/her sinful nature to YOUR cross and crucify them there. I pray that, he/she will live now by YOUR Holy Spirit, and I pray he/she will follow YOUR Holy Spirit's leading in every part of his/her life. I pray he/she will not become conceited or irritate others, or be jealous of others.

COLOSSIANS 3:11B-14

In this new life, it doesn't matter if we are a Jew or a Gentile, circumcised or uncircumcised, barbaric, uncivilized, slave, or free. I pray that to ---, YOU, Christ, are all that matters, and I PRAISE YOU, that YOU live in all of us. Since YOU, God, chose him/her to be YOUR holy people whom YOU love, I pray that he/she will clothe himself/herself with tenderhearted mercy, kindness, humility, gentleness, and patience. I pray that he/she will make allowance for another's faults and forgive the person who offends him/her. I pray he/she will remember that YOU, Lord, forgave him/her, so he/she must forgive others. And I pray he/she will wear the most important piece of clothing — that is love. YOUR love — that is what binds us all together in perfect harmony.

1 THESSALONIANS 5:13-15

I pray others will think highly of --- and give him/her their wholehearted love because of his/her work. And I pray that he/she will remember to live peaceably with each other. I pray he/she will warn others, as I pray he/she will not be those who are lazy. I pray he/she will encourage those who are timid. I pray he/she will take tender care of those who are weak. I pray he/she will be patient with everyone and will see that no one pays back evil for evil, but I pray he/she will always try to do good to each other and to everyone else.

11. *H*UMBLE

DEUTERONOMY 5:16

I pray that --- will honor my husband and I, his/her father and mother, as YOU, LORD, his/her God, have commanded him/her. Then I CLAIM YOUR PROMISE, that he/she will live a long, full life in the land that YOU, LORD, our God, will give him/her.

PROVERBS 22:4

I pray that YOU will richly bless --- with true humility and the fear of YOU, LORD. I CLAIM YOUR PROMISE, that these will lead him/her to riches, honor, and long life.

ZEPHANIAH 2:3

I pray --- will seek YOU, LORD, being the humble of the land; I pray he/she will do what YOU command. I pray he/she will always seek righteousness and seek humility, that perhaps he/she will be sheltered on the day of YOUR anger. (NIV)

12. *H*OLY SPIRIT:

1 CORINTHIANS 2:12

And I PRAISE YOU, that YOU, God, has actually given --- YOUR Spirit, not the world's spirit, so that he/she will know the wonderful things YOU, God, have freely given to him/her.

EPHESIANS 5:18-21

I pray that --- will not be drunk with wine, because that would ruin his/her life. Instead, I pray he/she will let YOUR Holy Spirit fill and control him/her. Then I PRAISE YOU, that he/she will sing psalms and hymns and spiritual songs among himself/herself, making music to YOU, Lord, in his/her heart. And I pray he/she will always give thanks for everything to YOU, God the Father, in the name of

YOU, our Lord Jesus Christ. And further, I pray also, that he/she will submit to another out of reverence for YOU, Christ.

JUDE: 20, 21

I pray that --- will continue to build his/her life on the foundation of his/her holy faith. And I pray he/she will continue to pray as he/she is directed by YOUR Holy Spirit. I pray that he/she will always live in such a way that YOUR love can bless him/her as he/she waits for the eternal life that YOU, our Lord Jesus Christ, in YOUR mercy is going to give him/her.

13. *I*NTEGRITY/ PURITY:

PSALM 25:20-21

I pray that YOU will protect ---! I pray YOU will rescue his/her life from them! I pray YOU will not let him/her be disgraced, for I pray he/she will trust in YOU. May integrity and honesty protect him/her, for I pray he/she will put his/her hope in YOU.

PSALM 26:1-8

I pray for ---, that YOU will declare him/her innocent, O, LORD, for I pray he/she will always act with integrity, and I pray he/she will trust in YOU, LORD, without wavering. I pray that YOU will put him/her on trial, LORD, and cross-examine him/her. I pray YOU will test his/her motives and affections. For I pray he/she will be constantly aware of YOUR unfailing love, and I pray he/she will live according to YOUR truth. I pray that he/she will not spend time with liars or go along with hypocrites. I pray he/she will hate the gathers of those who do evil, and I pray he/she will refuse to join in with the wicked. I pray he/she will wash his/her hands to declare his/her innocence. I pray he/she will come to YOUR altar, O, LORD, singing a song of thanksgiving and telling of all YOUR miracles. I pray that he/she will always love YOUR sanctuary, LORD, the place where YOUR glory shines.

PSALM 51:10-12

I pray that YOU will create in --- a clean heart, O, God. Renew a right spirit within him/her. I pray that YOU will not banish him/her from YOUR presence, and don't take YOUR Holy Spirit from him/her. I pray YOU will restore to him/her again the joy of YOUR salvation, and make him/her willing to obey YOU.

14. OY:

1 THESSALONIANS 5:16-22

I pray that --- will always be joyful. I pray he/she will keep on praying. No matter what happens, I pray that he/she will always be thankful, for this is YOUR will for him/her who belongs to YOU, Christ Jesus. I pray he/she will not stifle YOUR Holy Spirit. I pray he/she will not scoff at prophecies, but will test everything that is said. I pray he/she will always hold on to what is good and keep away from every kind of evil.

PSALM 5:11-12

I pray that --- will take refuge in YOU and that he/she will rejoice; I pray he/she will sing joyful praises forever. I pray that YOU will protect him/her, so he/she, who I pray will love YOUR name, may be filled with joy. For YOU PROMISE that YOU bless the godly, O, LORD, surrounding him/her with YOUR shield of love.

PSALM 19:8-11

I pray that --- will follow the commandments of YOU, LORD that are right, bringing joy to his/her heart. The commands of YOU, LORD are clear, giving insight to his/her life. I pray YOU will fill him/her with reverence for YOU, LORD, that is pure, lasting forever. The laws of YOU, LORD, are true; each one is fair. They, I pray are more desirable for him/her than gold, even the finest gold. I pray for him/her, that they are sweeter than honey, even honey dripping from the comb. I PRAISE YOU, that they are a warning to him/her who hears them, and that there is great reward for him/her who obeys them.

15. *K*NOWLEDGE/ WISDOM:

PROVERBS 29:3, 15

I pray that --- is the one who loves wisdom, that YOU PROMISE brings joy to his/her father, but I pray that he/she will not ever hang around with prostitutes, or his/her wealth is wasted. I pray he/she will receive the discipline and reprimand that produces wisdom, but I pray that I will not be a mother who is disgraced by an undisciplined child.

LUKE 2:51-52

Then, YOU returned to Nazareth with them and I pray --- will, as YOU were obedient to YOUR parents and YOUR mother, I pray that I, too, will store all these things in my heart. So, I pray he/she will, as YOU, Jesus, grew both in height and in wisdom, and I pray he/she will be, as YOU were, loved by God and by all who knew YOU.

EPHESIANS 1:17-19A

I am asking, that YOU, God, the glorious Father of our Lord Jesus Christ, will give --- spiritual wisdom and understanding. So that he/she will grow in his/her knowledge of YOU, God. I pray that his/her heart will be flooded with light so that he/she can understand the wonderful future that YOU have promised to those who YOU have called. I pray he/she will realize what a rich and glorious inheritance YOU have given to him/her, YOUR people. I pray that he/she will begin to understand the incredible greatness of YOUR power for him/her who believes YOU.

16. LOVE:

DEUTERONOMY 6:5 AND PHILIPPIANS 1:9-11

And I pray that --- will love YOU, LORD our God, with all his/her heart, all his/her soul, and all his/her strength. And I pray that his/her love for another will overflow more and more, and that he/she will keep on growing in his/her knowledge and understanding. For, I pray that he/she will understand what really matters, so that he/she will live a pure and blameless life until YOUR return! I pray that he/she will always be filled with the fruit of YOUR salvation, those good things that are produced in his/her life by YOU, Jesus Christ, for this will bring much glory and praise to YOU, God.

GALATIANS 5:5-6

I pray that --- will live by YOUR Spirit and eagerly wait to receive everything promised to him/her who is right with YOU, God, through faith. For I pray he/she will place his/her faith in YOU, Christ Jesus. It makes no difference to YOU, God, whether he/she is circumcised or not circumcised.

EPHESIANS 5:1-2

I pray that --- will follow YOUR example in everything he/she does, because he/she is YOUR dear child. I pray he/she will live a life filled with love for others, following the example of YOU, Christ, who loved him/her and gave YOURSELF as a sacrifice to take away our sins. And YOU, God, were pleased, because that sacrifice was like sweet perfume to YOU, as I pray will be his/hers.

17. MERCY/ FORGIVING:

PSALM 5:7-8

Because of YOUR unfailing love, I pray --- will enter YOUR house with deepest awe — I pray that he/she will worship at YOUR

Temple. I pray that YOU will lead him/her in the right path, O, Lord, or his/her enemies will conquer him/her. I pray YOU will tell him/her clearly what to do. And I pray YOU will show him/her which way to turn.

MATTHEW 5:7-9

I PRAISE YOU, that YOU, God, will bless ---, whom I pray will be merciful, for I CLAIM YOUR PROMISE, that he/she will be shown mercy. YOU, God, will bless him/her whose heart, I pray is pure, for I CLAIM YOUR PROMISE, that then — he/she will see YOU, God. YOU, God, will bless him/her, who I pray will work for peace, for he/she will be called the children of YOU, God.

JUDE 22-23

I pray that --- will always show mercy to those whose faith is wavering. I pray he/she will rescue others by snatching them from the flames of judgment. There are still others to whom I pray he/she will show mercy, but I pray he/she will be careful that he/she isn't contaminated by their sins.

18. NAME OF THE LORD:

PSALM 9:1-2, 9-10

I pray that --- will thank you, LORD, with all his/her heart; and I pray he/she will tell of all the marvelous things that YOU have done. I pray he/she will be filled with joy because of YOU. I pray he/she will sing praises to YOUR name, O, Most High. YOU, LORD, are a shelter for the oppressed, a refuge in times of trouble. I pray that he/she will know YOUR name and trust in YOU, for YOU, O, LORD, have never abandoned anyone. I pray that he/she searches for YOU.

PSALM 138:2-3

I pray that --- will bow before YOUR holy Temple as he/she worships. I pray he/she will give thanks to YOUR name for YOUR unfailing love and faithfulness, because YOUR promises are backed by all the honor of YOUR name. I that pray he/she will always pray and I PRAISE YOU, that YOU will answer him/her, and YOU will encourage him/her by giving him/her the strength he/she needs.

1 CORINTHIANS 1:2

As Paul wrote to the church of YOU, God, in Corinth, I pray for ---, who has been called by YOU, God, to be YOUR own holy people. I pray that YOU will make him/her holy by means of YOU, Christ Jesus, just as YOU did all Christians everywhere — I pray that he/she will call upon the name of YOU, Jesus Christ, our Lord.

19. OBEDIENT:

EXODUS 20:3, 6-8, 12-17

I pray that --- will not worship any other gods besides YOU. But YOU PROMISE that YOU lavish YOUR love on him/her who I pray will love YOU and obey YOUR commands, even for a thousand generations. I pray he/she will never misuse the name of YOU, LORD our God. YOU, LORD, would not let him/her go unpunished — if he/she were to misuse YOUR name. I pray that he/she will always remember to observe the Sabbath day by keeping it holy. I pray he/she will not covet his/he neighbor's house. I pray he/she will not covet his/her neighbor's wife, male or female servant, ox or donkey, or anything else his/her neighbor owns.

PROVERBS 6:20-24

My son, I pray that --- will obey his/her father's commands, and I pray he/she will not neglect my, his/her mother's, teaching. I pray he/she will keep YOUR words always in his/her heart. I pray he/she will tie them around his/her neck. Wherever he/she walks, their counsel will always lead him/her. When he/she sleeps, they will protect him/her. When he/she wakes up in the morning, they will advise him/her. For these commands and this teaching I pray he/she will use as a lamp to light the way ahead of him/her. I pray that he/she will have the correction of discipline that is the way to life. I pray he/she will be the young people who obey the law and are wise; not those who seek out worthless companions and bring shame to their parents.

TITUS 3:1-2

I pray that --- will submit to the government and its officers. I pray he/she will be obedient, always ready to do what is good. I pray he/she will not speak evil of anyone, and I pray he/she will avoid quarreling. Instead, I pray that he/she always will be gentle and show true humility to everyone.

20. PEACE:

ISAIAH 54:13

I pray that --- will be taught by YOU, LORD, and great will be our children's peace. (NIV)

1 THESSALONIANS 5:23-24

Now I pray for ---. May YOU, God of peace, make him/her holy in every way, and may his/her whole spirit and soul and body be kept blameless until that day when YOU, our Lord Jesus Christ, comes again.

ROMANS 3:5-6

I pray that --- is not dominated by the sinful nature that thinks about sinful things, but I pray he/she will be controlled by YOUR Holy Spirit and think about things that please YOUR Spirit. I pray his/her sinful nature will not control his/her mind, or there is death. But, I pray instead that YOUR Holy Spirit controls his/her mind, then, I CLAIM YOUR PROMISE, that there is life and peace for him/her.

21. *P*ERSEVERANCE:

2 PETER 1:3-8

I pray that --- will know YOU, Jesus, better. I PRAISE YOU, that then YOUR divine power will give him/her everything he/she needs for living a godly life. YOU have called him/her to receive YOUR own glory and goodness! And by that same mighty power, YOU have given him/her all of YOUR rich and wonderful promises. YOU have promised that he/she will escape the decadence all around him/her caused by evil desires and that he/she will share in YOUR divine nature. So I pray he/she will make every effort to apply the benefits of these promises to his/her life. Then his/her faith will produce a life of moral excellence. I pray he/she will have a life of moral excellence that leads to knowing YOU, God, better. Knowing YOU, God, leads to his/her self-control. Self-control leads to his/her patient endurance, and patient endurance leads to his/her godliness. Godliness leads to love for other Christians, and finally I pray he/she will grow to have genuine love for everyone. The more he/she will grow like this, the more he/she will become productive and useful in his/her knowledge of YOU, our Lord Jesus Christ.

HEBREWS 12:1-3

Therefore, since --- is surrounded by such a huge crowd of witnesses to his/her life of faith, I pray he/she will strip off every weight that slows him/her down, especially the sin that so easily hinders his/her progress. And I pray that he/she will run with endurance the race that YOU, God, have set before him/her. I pray he/she will do this by keeping his/her eyes on YOU, Jesus, on whom his/her faith depends from start to finish. YOU were willing to die a shameful death on the cross because of the joy YOU knew would be YOURS afterward. Now YOU are seated in the place of YOUR highest honor beside God's throne in heaven. I pray he/she will think about all YOU endured when sinful people did such terrible things to YOU, so that he/she won't become weary and give up.

ROMANS 5:3-4

I pray that --- will rejoice, too, when he/she runs into problems and trials, for I pray that he/she will know that they are good for him/her — they help him/her learn to endure. And endurance develops strength of character in him/her, and character strengthens his/her confident expectation of salvation.

22. *Q*UIET HEART/ SUBMISSIVE:

PROVERBS 13:1/15:5

I pray that --- will be a wise child who accepts our, his/her parent's, discipline, I pray that he/she will not be a young mocker who refuses to listen. I pray he/she will not be a fool who despises our discipline, and I pray that he/she will be one who learns from correction and is wise.

1 PETER 5:5-1

You, younger men, I pray that --- will accept the authority of the elders. And I pray that all of us will serve each other in humility, for YOU, God, set YOURself against the proud but YOU show favor to him/her who, I pray, is humble. So I pray that he/she will humble himself/herself under the mighty power of YOU, God, and in YOUR good time I CLAIM YOUR PROMISE, that YOU will honor him/her. I pray he/she will give all his/her worries and cares to YOU, God, for I pray that he/she will know that YOU care about what happens to him/her.

HEBREWS 12:9-15

I pray that --- will respect his/her earthly father who I pray will discipline him/her, and I pray that he/she will all the more cheerfully submit to the discipline of YOU, his/her heavenly Father and live forever. For I pray his/her earthly father will discipline him/her for a few years, doing his best. But I PRAISE YOU that YOUR discipline is always right and good for him/her because it means he/she will share in YOUR holiness. No discipline is enjoyable while it is happening — it is painful! But afterward, I PRAISE YOU that there will be quite a harvest of right living, for he/she who is trained in this way. So I pray that he/she will take a new grip with his/her tired hands and stand firm on his/her shaky legs and that he/she will mark out a straight path for his/her feet. Then those who follow him/her, though they are weak and lame, will not stumble and fall but will become strong. I pray he/she will try to live in peace with everyone, and seek to live a clean and holy life, for those who are not holy will not see YOU, Lord. I pray he/she will look after each other so that he/she will not miss out on the special favor of YOU, God. I pray, too, that he/she will watch out that no bitter root of unbelief rises up among him/her, for whenever it springs up, many are corrupted by its poison.

23. *R*EPENTANT:

DEUTERONOMY 30:2-3, 6

And when we and our children — I pray that --- will always return to YOU, LORD, our God, and obey YOU with all his/her heart and with all his/her soul, according to everything YOU command him/her today, then I CLAIM YOUR PROMISE, that YOU, LORD our God, will restore his/her fortunes and have compassion on him/her and will gather him/her again from all the nations where YOU scattered him/her. YOU, LORD our God, I pray will circumcise his/her heart and the hearts of his/her descendants so that he/she may love YOU with all his/her heart and with all his/her soul, and live. (NIV)

PROVERBS 28:13-14

I pray that --- will not cover over his/her sins and not prosper. But I pray that he/she will always confess and forsake them, and he/she will receive mercy. Blessed are those who I pray; he/she will have a tender conscience, but I pray he/she will not be the stubborn who are headed for serious trouble.

LUKE 3:8A

I pray that --- will prove by the way he/she lives that he/she has really turned from his/her sins and turned to YOU, God. I pray that he/she will not just say, he's/she's safe —he's/she's the descendants of Abraham. That proves nothing. YOU, God, can change these stones here into children of Abraham.

24. *S*PIRIT/ SELF-CONTROLLED:

1 PETER 1:13-16

So, I pray that --- will think clearly and exercise self-control. I pray he/she will look forward to the special blessing that will come to him/her at the return of YOU, Jesus Christ. I pray that he/she will obey YOU, God, because I pray he/she will know he/she is YOUR child. I pray he/she will not slip back into his/her old ways of doing evil; he/she didn't know any better then. But now I pray he/she will be holy in everything he/she does, just as YOU, God, — who chose him/her to be YOUR children — is holy.

1 PETER 5:8-9

I pray that --- will be careful! I pray he/she will watch out for attacks from the devil, his/her great enemy. He prowls around like a roaring lion, looking for some victim to devour. I pray that he/she will take a firm stand against him, and be strong in his/her faith. I pray that he/she will remember that his/her Christian brothers and sisters all over the world are going through the same kind of suffering he/she is.

1 THESSALONIANS 5:8, 11

But I pray that --- will live in the light and think clearly, protected by his/her body armor of faith and love, and I pray that he/she will wear as his/her helmet the confidence of YOUR salvation. So I pray he/she will encourage each other and build each other up, just as I pray he/she is already doing.

25. *S*ERVANT'S HEART:

1 TIMOTHY 5:4

But, I pray for my children and/or grandchildren. I pray for ---, that as his/her first responsibility is to show godliness at home and I pray he/she will repay us, his/her parents by taking care of us. This is something that pleases YOU, God, very much.

MATTHEW 25:21

I pray, that YOU, ---'s Master, will reply, Well done, as I pray that he/she will be YOUR good and faithful servant! I pray he/she will be faithful with a few things, and that then YOU will put him/her in charge of many things. I pray he/she will come and share in YOUR, his/her Master's, happiness! (NIV)

COLOSSIANS 3:23

I pray that --- will work hard and cheerfully at whatever he/she does, as though he/she is working for YOU, Lord, rather than for people.

26. *T*HANKFUL/ GRATEFUL:

COLOSSIANS 3:15-17

And I pray that --- will let the peace that comes from YOU, Christ, rule in his/her hearts. For as members of one body he/she is called to live in peace. And, I pray that he/she will always be thankful. I pray he/she will let the word of YOU, Christ, in all their richness, live in his/her heart and make him/her wise. I pray he/she will use YOUR words to teach and counsel each other. I pray he/she will sing psalms and hymns and spiritual songs to YOU, God, with a thankful heart. And I pray that whatever he/she does or says, let it be as a representative of YOU, Lord Jesus, all the while giving thanks through YOU to God the Father.

PSALM 9:1-2 AND EPHESIANS 5:20

I pray that --- will thank you, LORD, with all his/her heart; that he/she will tell of all the marvelous things that YOU have done. I pray that YOU will fill him/her with joy and that he/she will sing praises to YOUR name, O, Most High. And I pray that he/she will always give thanks for everything to YOU, God the Father, in the name of YOU, our Lord Jesus Christ.

COLOSSIANS 2:6-7

And now, just as I pray that --- has accepted YOU, Christ Jesus, as his/her Lord, I pray he/she will continue to live in obedience to YOU. I pray he/she will let his/her roots grow down into YOU and draw up nourishment from YOU, so that he/she will grow in faith, strong and vigorous in the truth that I pray he/she will always be taught. I pray also, that his/her life will overflow with thanksgiving for all that YOU have done.

27. UNDERSTAND/ SEEK YOUR WILL:

JEREMIAH 33:2-3

YOU LORD, the maker of the heavens and earth — the LORD is YOUR name. I pray that --- will always ask YOU and I CLAIM YOUR PROMISE that YOU will tell him/her some remarkable secrets about what is going to happen here.

ISAIAH 11:2

And I pray for ---, that the Spirit of YOU, LORD, will rest on him/her — YOUR Spirit of wisdom and understanding, YOUR Spirit of counsel and might, YOUR Spirit of knowledge and the fear of YOU, LORD.

COLOSSIANS 1:9-10

So I have continued praying for --- ever since we first heard about him/her. I pray for him/her, asking YOU, God, to give him/her a complete understanding of what YOU want to do in his/her life, and I ask YOU to make him/her wise with spiritual wisdom. Then the way that he/she lives will always honor and please YOU, Lord, and I pray he/she will continually do good, kind things for others. All the while I pray he/she will always learn to know YOU, God, better and better.

28. *U*PRIGHT/ HOLY:

LEVITICUS 19:1-3

As, YOU, LORD also said to Moses, Say this to the entire communi-ty of Israel: I pray that --- will be holy because YOU, LORD, his/her God, YOU are holy. I pray that he/she will always show respect for his/her mother and father, and I pray he/she will always observe YOUR Sabbath days of rest, for YOU, LORD, are his/her God.

PROVERBS 23:19-26

For my child, I pray that --- will always listen and be wise. I pray he/she will keep his/her heart on the right course. I pray he/she will not carouse with drunkards and gluttons, for they are on their way to poverty. Too much sleep clothes a person with rags. I pray he/she will listen to his/her father, who gave him/her life, and I pray he/she will not despise my, his/her mother's, experience when I am old. I pray that he/she will get the truth and won't ever sell it; also I pray he/she will get wisdom, discipline, and discernment. Then, I PRAISE YOU, that my husband, his/her father of godly children, has cause for joy. What a pleasure it is to have wise children. So I pray he/she will always give us, his/her parents, joy! May I who gave him/her birth be happy. O, I pray that my son/daughter, will give YOU, his/her heart. May his/her eyes always delight in YOUR ways of wisdom.

PROVERBS 21:21

I pray that --- always pursues godliness and unfailing love and, I CLAIM YOUR PROMISE, that he/she will find life, godliness, and honor.

29. *V*ICTORIOUS:

PSALM 20:4-5

I pray that YOU will grant ---'s heart's desire and fulfill all his/her plans. We will shout for joy when we hear of his/her victory, flying banners to honor YOU, our God. May YOU, LORD, answer all his/her prayers.

2 TIMOTHY 1:7

For YOU, God, have not given --- a spirit of fear and timidity, but I pray he/she will live by YOUR SPIRIT of power, love, and self-discipline.

MATTHEW 25:21

YOU, ---'s Master, I pray will always be full of praise. Well done, I pray he/she will hear, as YOUR good and faithful servant. I pray he/she will be faithful in handling this small amount, so now YOU, will give him/her many more responsibilities. I pray he/she will always be able to celebrate together with YOU!

30. *Y*OUR WORD:

1 SAMUEL 2:21, 26/3:10, 19

And as YOU, LORD, gave Hannah three sons and two daughters. As Samuel did, I pray that --- will grow up in the presence of YOU, LORD. As young Samuel, as he/she grows taller, I pray he/she will continue to gain favor with YOU, LORD, and with the people. And YOU, LORD, I pray will come and call to him/her as YOU did,

"Samuel! Samuel!" Then, as Samuel said, I pray he/she will always respond to YOU, "Speak, for YOUR servant is listening." As Samuel, I pray that as he/she grows up, that YOU, LORD, will be with him/her, and I pray that everything he/she says is wise and helpful.

PSALM 119:9-11

How can a young person, I pray that --- will stay pure? I pray he/she will obey YOUR word and follow its rules. I pray he/she will always try his/her best to find YOU — I pray YOU will not let him/her wander from YOUR commands. I pray he/she will hide YOUR word in his/her heart, that he/she might not sin against YOU.

PROVERBS 7:1-3

I pray that --- will always follow YOUR and our advice. I pray he/she will always treasure YOUR commands. I pray he/she will obey them and then I PRAISE YOU that he/she will live! I pray he/she will guard YOUR teachings as his/her most precious possession. I pray he/she will tie them on his/her finger as a reminder. I pray that he/she will write them deep within his/her heart.

31. *Z*EALOUS/ FEAR LORD:

PROVERBS 23:17, 19-20

I pray that --- will not envy sinners, but will always continue to fear YOU, Lord. I pray that he/she, my child, will always listen and be wise. I pray he/she will always keep his/her heart on the right course. I pray he/she will not ever carouse with drunkards and gluttons

PROVERBS 24:21

I pray that --- my child, will always fear YOU, our LORD and the king, and I pray he/she will not ever associate with rebels.

2 TIMOTHY 2:21-22

I pray that --- will keep himself/herself pure, that he/she will be a utensil that YOU, God, can use for YOUR purpose. I pray his/her life will be clean, and I pray he/she will be ready for YOU, his/her Master to use him/her for every good work. I pray he/she will run from anything that stimulates youthful lust. I pray he/she will always follow anything that makes him/her want to do right. I pray he/she will always pursue faith and love and peace, and enjoy the companionship of those who call on YOU, Lord, with pure hearts.

31 DAYS
of
"ALPHABET PRAYERS"
For Your Pastors

The elders who direct
the affairs of the
church well are worthy
of double honor,
especially those whose work is
preaching and teaching.

1 TIMOTHY 5:17

DAILY: ASK GOD'S HEDGE OF
PROTECTION & FILLING OF HIS SPIRIT

1. $\mathscr{A}$BIDE:

1 JOHN 4:16-18 AND JOHN 15:5

And so we know and I pray that Pastor will rely on the love that YOU, God, have for him. YOU are love. I pray he will live in love, living in YOU, and YOU, God, in him. In this way, love is made complete among him so that he will have confidence on the Day of Judgment, because in this world I pray he will be like YOU. There is no fear in love. But I pray he will live in YOUR perfect love that will drive out his fear, because fear has to do with punishment. The one who fears is not made perfect in love. Yes, YOU are the vine; we are the branches. I pray that Pastor will remain in YOU, and YOU in him, for YOU PROMISE he will produce much fruit. For apart from YOU, he can do nothing.

2. $\mathscr{B}$LESSED:

GENESIS 12:2-3 AND NUMBERS 6:24-26

I pray YOU will make PASTOR into a great nation and that YOU will bless him; I pray YOU will make his name great, and that he will be a blessing. I pray YOU will bless those who bless him, and curse those who curse him; I pray that all peoples on earth (and our congregation) will be blessed through him. And I pray may YOU, LORD, bless Pastor and protect him. May YOU, LORD, smile on him and be gracious to him. May YOU, LORD, show him YOUR favor and give him YOUR peace.

3. $\mathscr{C}$OMMISSION:

ACTS 20:24, 26-28 AND 2 THESSALONIANS 1:11-12

I pray that Pastor will consider his life worth nothing unless he continues to use it for doing the work assigned him by YOU, Lord Jesus, the work of telling others the Good News about YOUR wonderful kindness and love. Let him be able to say plainly that he has been faithful to YOU. I pray no one's damnation can be blamed on him, for I pray he will not ever shrink from declaring all that YOU want for us. And I pray he will beware! I pray he will be sure to feed and shepherd YOUR flock, YOUR church, purchased with YOUR blood, over whom the Holy Spirit has appointed Pastor as our over-seer. I pray that YOU will raise up many to keep on praying for Pastor, that YOU, our God, will make him worthy of the life to which YOU have called him. And I pray that YOU, God, by YOUR power, will fulfill all his good intentions and faithful deeds. Then, I pray that everyone will give honor to YOUR name, our Lord Jesus, because of him, and that YOU will be honored along with Pastor. I pray this will all be made possible because I pray YOU will show him the undeserved favor of YOU, our God, and our Lord Jesus Christ.

4. CONTENT:

1 TIMOTHY 6, 8-9, 11-12, 17-18

I pray that YOU will bless Pastor with godliness with contentment that is great gain. But if he has food and clothing, I pray he will be content with that. I pray he will not be those who want to get rich and fall into temptation and I pray YOU will protect him from falling into a trap and into many foolish and harmful desires that plunge men into ruin and destruction. But I pray that Pastor, being a man of God, will flee from all of this and pursue righteousness, godliness, faith, love, endurance and gentleness. I pray he will fight the good fight of the faith. Taking hold of the eternal life to which he has been called. I pray he will command those who are rich in this present world not to be arrogant nor to put their hope in wealth, which is so uncertain, but to put their hope in YOU, God. I pray he will command us to do good, to be rich in good deeds, and to be generous and willing to share.

5. *D*EVOTED:

COLOSSIANS 4:2-5 AND PSALM 37:5-7A

I pray that Pastor will devote himself to prayer, being watchful and thankful. And I pray that YOU, God, will open up the door for his message, so that he may proclaim the mystery of YOU, Christ, for which he is in chains. I pray that he may proclaim it clearly, as he should. I pray that he will be wise in the way he acts towards outsiders and will always make the most of every opportunity. I pray that Pastor will commit everything he does to YOU, LORD. I pray he will trust YOU, and YOU PROMISE YOU will help him. YOU, I pray, will make his innocence as clear as the dawn, and the justice for his cause, I pray, will shine like the noonday sun. I pray he will be still in the presence of YOU, LORD, and wait patiently for YOU to act, as he I pray will devote himself to YOU.

6. *E*VEN-TEMPERED:

PROVERBS 17:27; 1 TIMOTHY 3:2-4 AND TITUS 2:2

I pray that Pastor will be a truly wise person who uses few words; and I pray he will be a person with understanding that is even-tempered. I pray that Pastor will be a man whose life cannot be spoken against. I pray he will be faithful to his wife. I pray he will always exhibit self-control, live wisely, and have a good reputation. I pray he will enjoy having guests in his home and he, I pray, will be able to teach. I pray he will not be a heavy drinker or be violent. He, I pray, will always be gentle, peace loving and not one who loves money. I pray also that Pastor will manage his own family well, and I pray he will have children who respect and obey him. I pray he will also teach the older men to be, as himself, temperate, worthy of respect, self-controlled, and sound in faith, in love and in endurance.

7. $\mathscr{F}$AITH:

2 CORINTHIANS 4:16-18; 5:7 AND JOHN 14:12-14

I pray Pastor does not lose heart. Though outwardly he is wasting away, yet inwardly I pray, he will be renewed day by day. For his light and momentary troubles are achieving for him an eternal glory that far outweighs them all. So I pray he will fix his eyes not on what is seen, but on what is unseen. For what is seen is temporary, but what is unseen is eternal. I pray that YOU will enable him to live by faith, not by sight. I pray also, that Pastor will believe the truth is, he who believes in YOU will do the same works YOU have done, and even greater works, because YOU, Jesus, have gone to be with YOUR Father. Bless him with the faith that believes he can ask for anything in YOUR name, and YOU will do it, because the work of YOU, the Son, brings glory to YOUR Father. Yes, I pray Pastor will have faith to ask anything in YOUR name and YOU will do it.

8. $\mathscr{F}$ILLED:

COLOSSIANS 1:9-10; EPHESIANS 5:18-21
AND HEBREWS 13:20-21

I pray Pastor will not be drunk with wine, because that will ruin his life. Instead, I pray he will let YOUR Holy Spirit fill and control him. Then I pray he will sing psalms and hymns and spiritual songs, making music to YOU, Lord, in his heart. And I pray he will always give thanks for everything to YOU, God the Father, in the name of our Lord Jesus Christ. And further, I pray he will submit to one another out of reverence for YOU, Christ. I pray for Pastor asking YOU, God, to fill him with the knowledge of YOUR will through all spiritual wisdom and understanding. I pray this in order that he may live a life worthy of YOU, Lord, and may please YOU in every way: bearing fruit in every good work and growing in his knowledge of YOU. May YOU, God of peace, who through the blood of the eternal covenant brought back from the dead our Lord Jesus, YOU, that great Shepherd of the sheep, equip Pastor with everything good for doing YOUR will, and may YOU work in him what is pleasing to YOU through Jesus Christ, to whom be glory for ever and ever. Amen.

9. GENTLE:

GALATIANS 5:16, 22-26 AND
COLOSSIANS 3:11B-14

I pray that Pastor will live according to his new life in YOUR Holy Spirit. Then he won't be doing what his sinful nature craves. But when YOUR Holy Spirit, I pray, will control his life, YOU will produce this kind of fruit in him: love, joy, peace, patience, kindness, goodness, faithfulness, gentleness, and self-control. Here there is no conflict with the law. Those who belong to YOU, Christ Jesus, I pray he daily, will nail the passions and desires of his sinful nature to YOUR cross and will crucify them there. I pray he will be living now by YOUR Holy Spirit, and I pray he will follow YOUR Holy Spirit's leading in every part of his life. I pray he will not become conceited or irritate another, or be jealous of another. In this new life, it doesn't matter if you are a Jew or a Gentile, circumcised or uncircumcised, barbaric, uncivilized, slave, or free. I pray for Pastor, that YOU, Christ, are all that matters, and YOU live in all of us. Since YOU, God, have chosen him to be YOUR holy people whom YOU love, I pray he will clothe himself with YOUR tenderhearted mercy, kindness, humility, gentleness, and patience. I pray he will make allowance for each other's faults and forgive the person who offends him. I pray he will always remember that YOU, Lord, forgave him, so he must forgive others. And the most important piece of clothing I pray he will wear is love. YOUR love is what binds us all together in perfect harmony.

10. *H*UMBLE:

PROVERBS 22:1, 3-4; 29:23 AND 1 PETER 5:6-7

I pray that Pastor will choose a good reputation over great riches, for being held in high esteem is better than having silver or gold. I pray he will be a prudent person who foresees the danger ahead and takes precautions; I pray he will not be the simpleton who goes blindly on and suffers the consequences. I pray YOU will bless him with true humility and fear of YOU, LORD, that will lead him to riches, honor and long life. I pray for Pastor, I pray YOU will cast out all pride that ends in humiliation, while I pray YOU will bless him with humility that brings him honor. So I pray that Pastor will always humble himself under the mighty power of YOU, God, and in YOUR good time I CLAIM YOUR PROMISE, YOU will honor him. And, I pray he will always give all his worries and cares to YOU, God, for I pray he will know YOU care about what happens to him.

11. *H*OLY:

HEBREWS 12.14A AND TITUS 1.6-9, 2.1, 7-8, 12, 15

I pray that Pastor will try to live at peace with everyone, and seek to live a holy and clean life. I pray that he will be blameless, the husband of but one wife, a man whose children believe and are not open to the charge of being wild and disobedient. Since he is an overseer, entrusted with YOUR work, I pray he will be blameless — not overbearing, quick tempered, or given to drunkenness, not violent, not pursuing dishonest gain. Rather, I pray he will be hospitable, one who loves what is good, and who is self-controlled, upright, holy and disciplined. I pray he will hold firmly to YOUR trustworthy message, so that he can encourage others by sound doctrine and refute those who oppose it. I pray he will teach what is in accord with sound doctrine. In everything I pray he will set us an example by doing what is good. In his teaching, I pray he will show integrity, seriousness and soundness of speech that cannot be condemned, so that those who oppose him may be ashamed because they have nothing bad to say about him. I pray he will say "no" to ungodliness and worldly passions, and I pray he will live a self-controlled, upright and godly life in this present age. These then, are also the things I pray he will teach. I also pray that Pastor will encourage and rebuke with all authority and I pray he will not let anyone despise him.

12. *I*NTEGRITY:

PROVERBS 13:6 AND PSALM 25:20-21; 26:1-8

I pray for Pastor, pour out YOUR SPIRIT of Righteousness that guards Pastor, who I pray will always be a man of integrity, but I pray he will not be touched by wickedness that overthrows the sinner. I pray YOU will always protect him! I pray YOU will rescue his life from them! I pray YOU will not let him be disgraced, for I pray he will always trust in you. May integrity and honesty protect him, for I pray he will put his hope in YOU, God. I pray for Pastor, that YOU will declare him innocent, O, LORD, for I pray he will always act with integrity. I pray he will trust in YOU, LORD, without wavering. I pray YOU will put him on trial, LORD, and cross-examine him. I pray YOU will test his motives and affections. For I pray he will be constantly aware of your unfailing love, and I pray he will always live according to your truth. I pray also that he will not spend time with liars or go along with hypocrites. I pray he will hate the gathers of those who do evil, and I pray he will refuse to join in with the wicked. I pray he will wash his hands to declare his innocence. I pray he always will come to your altar, O, LORD, singing a song of thanksgiving and telling of all your miracles. I pray he shall love your sanctuary, LORD, the place where your glory shines.

13. *J*OY:

PSALM 28:7   1 THESSALONIANS 5:16-25
AND PSALM 16:11

I pray YOU, LORD, will always be Pastor's strength, his shield from every danger. I pray he will trust in YOU with all his heart. As I pray YOU always help him, may his heart be filled with joy. I pray today that he will burst out in songs of thanksgiving. I pray that Pastor will be joyful always, that he will pray continually, and that he will give thanks in all circumstances, for this is YOUR will for him in Christ Jesus. I pray he will not put out the Spirit's fire, and he will not treat prophecies with contempt. I pray he will test everything and hold on to everything that is good. I pray he will avoid every kind of evil. May YOU, God, YOURSELF, the God of peace, sanctify Pastor through and through. May his whole spirit, soul, and body be kept blameless at the coming of YOU, our Lord Jesus Christ. I praise YOU — the one who calls him is faithful and YOU will do it. I pray also that many brothers will pray for him. I pray YOU will make known to Pastor the path of life, that YOU will fill him with joy in YOUR presence and with eternal pleasures at your right hand.

14. *K*IND:

THESSALONIANS 5:13-15; EPHESIANS 4:26-27,
29-32 AND 2 TIMOTHY 2:25-26

I pray others will think highly of Pastor and give him their whole-hearted love because of his work. And I pray he remembers to live peaceably with others. I pray he warns those who are lazy. I pray he encourages those who are timid and that he takes tender care of those who are weak. I pray he will be patient with everyone and that he will see that no one pays back evil for evil, but I pray he will always encourage us to try to do good to each other and to everyone else. I pray also for Pastor that in his anger he will not sin: that he will not let the sun go down while he is still angry, and that he will not let the devil get a foothold. I pray he will not let any unwholesome talk come out of his mouth, but only what is helpful for building others up according to their needs, that it may benefit those who listen. And I pray he will not grieve the Holy Spirit of YOU, God, with whom he has been sealed for the day of redemption. I pray he will get rid of all bitterness, rage, anger, brawling and slander, along with every form of malice. I pray he will be kind and compassionate to others, forgiving others, just as in Christ, God, YOU have forgiven him. I pray he will gently teach those who oppose the truth, and I pray YOU, God, will change those people's hearts, and that they will believe the truth, and that they will come to their senses and escape the trap of the devil who has taken them captive to do his will.

15. KNOWLEDGE:

EPHESIANS 1:17-20; COLOSSIANS 1:9-10 AND 2 PETER 3:18

I am asking YOU, God, the glorious Father of our Lord Jesus Christ, to give Pastor spiritual wisdom and understanding so that he will grow in his knowledge of YOU, God. I pray that his heart will be flooded with light so that he can understand the wonderful future YOU have promised to those, including him, whom YOU have called. I pray he will realize what a rich and glorious inheritance YOU have given to him, and all YOUR people. I pray that he will begin to understand the incredible greatness of YOUR power for him, and us who believe YOU. I pray he will experience this is the same mighty power that raised Christ from the dead and seated him in the place of honor at YOUR right hand in the heavenly realms. I pray for Pastor asking YOU, God, to fill him with the knowledge of YOUR will through all spiritual wisdom and understanding. I pray this in order that he may live a life worthy of YOU, Lord, and may please YOU in every way: bearing fruit in every good work and growing in his knowledge of YOU. And I pray that Pastor will grow in the grace and knowledge of YOU, our Lord and Savior Jesus Christ. To YOU be glory both now and forever! Amen.

16. $\mathscr{L}$OVE:

PHILIPPIANS 1:9-11; 1 JOHN 4:16;
MARK 12:30-31; COLOSSIANS 3:19, 21
AND 1 CORINTHIANS 13:4-7

And this is my prayer: that Pastor's love may abound more and more in knowledge and depth of insight, so that he may be able to discern what is best and may be pure and blameless until the day of YOU, Jesus Christ. I pray he will be filled with the fruit of righteousness that comes through YOU, Jesus Christ, to the glory and praise of YOU, God. And I pray that Pastor will know and rely on the love YOU, God, have for him. And I pray Pastor will love YOU, Lord our God, with all his heart, all his soul, all his mind, and all his strength. The second is equally important; I pray he will love his neighbor as himself. YOU tell us no other commandment is greater that these. And I pray that Pastor, as a husband, will love his wife and never treat her harshly. If he does, she would become discouraged and quit trying. I pray YOU will bless Pastor and his family with YOUR love that is patient, and love that is kind. I pray his love does not envy, it does not boast, it is not proud. It is not rude, it is not self-seeking, it is not easily angered, and it keeps no record of wrongs. I pray he will be filled with love that does not delight in evil but rejoices with the truth. Please bless him with love that always protects, always trusts, always hopes, and always perseveres.

17. $\mathscr{M}$ERCY:

MATTHEW 5:6-7; HEBREW 4:16 AND JUDE 20-25

I pray for Pastor, that YOU will bless him who, I pray, he will be hungry and thirsty for justice for he will receive it in full. YOU bless those who, I pray, he will be merciful, for he also will be shown mercy. So I pray Pastor will come boldly to YOUR throne — our gracious God. There YOU PROMISE, he will receive YOUR mercy, and he will find grace to help him when we need it. I pray also, that Pastor will build himself up in his most holy faith and pray in YOUR Holy Spirit. I pray he will keep himself in YOUR love as we wait for the mercy of YOU, our Lord Jesus Christ, to bring him to eternal life. I pray he will be merciful to those who doubt; snatching others from the fire and saving them. To others I pray he will show mercy mixed with fear, hating even the clothing stained by corrupted flesh. To YOU who is able to keep him from falling and to present Pastor before YOUR glorious presence without fault and with great joy — to YOU, the only God, our Savior, be glory, majesty, power and authority, through YOU, Jesus Christ our Lord, before all ages, now and forever! Amen.

18. $\mathscr{M}$ESSAGE:

2 THESSALONIANS 3:1-3, 5, 16, 18;

1 THESSALONIANS 1:5-6; 2:4-8, 10-13

AND 1 CORINTHIANS 2:2-4

I pray that many dear brothers and sisters will pray for Pastor. And I pray that YOUR message, our Lord, will spread rapidly and be honored wherever it goes, just as when it came to him. And I pray, too, that Pastor will be saved from wicked and evil people, for not everyone believes YOU, Lord. But I thank you that YOU, Lord, are faithful; and that YOU will make Pastor strong and guard him from the evil one. May YOU, Lord, bring him into an ever deeper understanding of the love of God and the endurance that comes from YOU, Christ. May YOU, the Lord of peace, YOURSELF always give Pastor YOUR peace no matter what happens. I pray that YOU, Lord, will be with him. May YOUR grace, Lord Jesus, be with him and us all. And I pray that when Pastor preaches the gospel, it will come to us not simply with words, but also with YOUR power, with YOUR Holy Spirit and with deep conviction. And may we know how he lives among us for our sakes. I pray that we may become imitators of Pastor and of YOU, Lord. In spite of any severe suffering, may we welcome his message with the joy given by YOUR Holy Spirit. And I pray that Pastor will speak as a man approved by YOU, God, being entrusted with the gospel. I pray that he will not try to please men but YOU, God, who tests his heart. I pray he will never use flattery, nor will he put on a mask to cover up greed —YOU, God, are his witness. I pray he will not be looking for praise from men, not from others or anyone else. As an apostle of YOU, Christ, he could have been a burden to us, but I pray he will always be gentle among us, like a mother caring for her little children. I pray he will love us so much that he will be delighted to share with us not only the gospel of YOU, God, but his life as well, because I pray we will become so dear to him. I pray we will be witnesses, and so are YOU, God, of how holy, righteous and blameless I pray Pastor is among us who, I pray, will believe. I pray he will always deal with each of us as a father deals with his own children. I pray YOU will give Pastor the grace to be encouraging, comforting and urging us to live lives worthy of YOU, God, who calls us into YOUR kingdom and glory. And I also pray and thank YOU, God, continually, because when we receive the word of YOU, God, which we hear from Pastor, I pray and thank you that we will accept it not as the word of men, but as it actually is, the word of YOU, God, which is at work in us, his flock who I pray will always believe. And I pray that Pastor will resolve to know nothing while he is with us except YOU, Jesus Christ, and YOU crucified. As he comes to us in weakness and fear, and with much trembling, I pray that his message and preaching will not be with wise and persuasive words, but with a demonstration of YOUR Spirit's power, so that our faith might not rest on men's wisdom, but on YOUR power!

PLEASE REMEMBER to TAKE SOME TIME
to PRAISE GOD FOR and PRAY FOR:
ALL of YOUR PASTORS, ELDERS,
DEACONS, TEACHERS, LEADERS,
PRAYER TEAMS, MUSIC MINISTERS,
STAFF, NURSERY WORKERS,
VOLUNTEERS and THEIR FAMILIES.
PRAY that GOD WILL SHOW YOU
PERSONALLY, HOW YOU CAN HELP
and ENCOURAGE YOUR PASTOR
WITH a NOTE, PHONE CALL, EMAIL,
DINNER, or BAKED GOODS.
THEY NEED OUR ENCOURAGEMENT
and LOVE EXPRESSED THROUGHOUT
the ENTIRE YEAR — LET'S MAKE THIS
a PASTOR APPRECIATION YEAR!
BE CREATIVE and WILLING TO
SACRIFICE LOVE, MONEY, and TIME.

19. NOBLE:

PSALM 32:1-2; ISAIAH 32:8;
PHILIPPIANS 4:8-9 AND 2 PETER 1:5-8

Oh, what joy for Pastor, whose rebellion is forgiven, I pray YOU will keep him repentant, whose sin is put out of sight! Yes, what joy for him whose record YOU, LORD, have cleared of sin. I pray his life will be lived in complete honesty! And I pray Pastor will be a good person and that he will be generous to others and then, he will be blessed for all he does. So I pray Pastor will make every effort to apply the benefits of these, YOUR promises, to his life. Then his faith will produce a life of moral excellence. I pray YOU will bless him with a life of moral excellence that leads to knowing YOU, God, better. Knowing YOU, God, leads to his self-control. I pray YOU will bless him with self-control that leads to his godliness. Godliness leads to his love for other Christians, and finally I pray he will grow to have genuine love for everyone. The more he grows like this, the more I pray he will become productive and useful in his knowledge of YOU, our Lord Jesus Christ. And now, I pray Pastor will fix his thoughts on what is true and honorable and right. I pray he will think about things that are pure and lovely and admirable. I pray he will think about things that are excellent and worthy of praise, and I pray he will keep putting into practice all he has learned from YOU and heard from YOU and saw YOU doing, and I pray that YOU, God of peace, will be with him.

20. BEY:

DEUTERONOMY 6:1-6 AND 1 JOHN 3:21-23

I pray that Pastor will teach and obey all the commands, decrees and laws that YOU, LORD our God, directed Moses to teach us to observe in the land we are about to enter and occupy, and so I pray he and his children and grandchildren might fear YOU, LORD our God, as long as they live. I pray he will obey all YOUR laws and commands, that he will enjoy a long life. I pray he will listen closely to everything YOU say. I pray he will always be careful to obey. Then all will go well with him, and he will have many children in the land flowing with milk and honey, just as YOU, LORD, the God of our ancestors, promised him. I pray he will Hear, O, Israel! YOU, Lord, are his God — YOU, Lord, alone. And he, I pray, will love YOU, Lord his God, with all his heart, all his soul, and all his strength. And I pray he will commit himself wholeheartedly to these commands YOU are giving him today. And I pray Pastor will have a clear conscience, so he can come to YOU, God, with bold confidence. And I praise YOU that then he will receive whatever he requests because he, I pray, will always obey YOU and do the things that please YOU.

21. *P*OWER:

ISAIAH 11:2-3A; 50:4-5 AND
EPHESIANS 5:10-11, 15-17; 6:10-11, 19

I pray YOUR Spirit, Lord, will rest on Pastor YOUR Spirit of wisdom and understanding, YOUR Spirit of counsel and of power, YOUR Spirit of knowledge and of the fear of YOU, Lord, and I pray he will delight in the fear of YOU, Lord. YOU, Sovereign Lord, I pray will give him an instructed tongue, to know the word that sustains the weary. YOU, I pray, will awaken him morning by morning, waken his ear to listen like one being taught. YOU, Sovereign Lord, I pray will open his ears. I pray he will find out what pleases YOU, Lord. And he will have nothing to do with the fruitless deeds of darkness, but rather expose them. And he will be very careful then, how he lives — not as unwise, but as wise, making the most of every opportunity, because the days are evil. I pray he will not be foolish, but understand what YOUR will is. I pray he will be strong in YOU, Lord, and in YOUR mighty power. I pray he will put on the full armor of YOU, God, so that he can take his stand against the devil's schemes. And I pray that whenever he opens his mouth, words may be given him so that he will make known the mystery of the gospel.

22. $\mathscr{P}$URE:

PSALM 51:1-4, 10-12, 13, 17
AND 2 TIMOTHY 2:21-22

Have mercy on Pastor according to YOUR unfailing love; according to YOUR great compassion, blot out his transgressions. Wash away all his iniquity and cleanse him from his sin. For I pray he will know and acknowledge his transgressions, and his sin that is always before him. Against YOU, and YOU only has he sinned and done what is evil in YOUR sight, so that YOU are proved right when YOU speak and justified when YOU judge. Create in Pastor a pure heart, O, God, and renew a steadfast spirit within him. Do not cast him from YOUR presence or take YOUR Holy Spirit from him. Restore to him the joy of YOUR salvation and grant him a willing spirit to sustain him. Then he will teach transgressors YOUR ways, and sinners will turn back to YOU. The sacrifice of YOU, God, is Pastor's broken spirit; his broken and contrite heart, O, God, YOU will not despise. And I pray Pastor will keep himself pure, that he will be a utensil YOU, God, can use for YOUR purpose. I pray his life will be clean, and I pray he will always be ready for YOU, his Master, to use him for every good work. I pray he will run from anything that stimulates youthful lust. I pray he will always follow anything that makes him want to do right. I pray Pastor will always pursue faith, love and peace, and enjoy the companionship of those who call on YOU, Lord, with pure hearts.

23. $\mathscr{Q}$UIET:

PSALM 131:1-3; 23:1-3, 6; ZEPHANIAH 3:17,13B
AND PHILIPPIANS 4:6-7

LORD, I pray Pastor's heart is not proud; his eyes are not haughty. I pray he will not concern himself with matters too great or awesome for him. But I pray he will have stilled and quieted himself, just as a small child is quiet with its mother. Yes, like a small child, I pray his soul is within him. O, Israel, I pray he will put his hope in YOU, LORD, — now and always. YOU, LORD, are his Shepherd; he shall not be in want. I pray YOU shall make him lie down in green pastures, YOU will lead him beside quiet waters, and YOU shall restore his soul. YOU, I pray, will guide him in paths of righteousness for YOUR name's sake. Surely, I pray, goodness and love will follow Pastor all the days of his life, and he will dwell in YOUR house, LORD, forever. And I pray Pastor will know that YOU, LORD our God, are with him, YOU are mighty to save. YOU, I pray, will take great delight in him, YOU will quiet him with YOUR love, YOU will rejoice over him with singing, and I pray he will eat and lie down and no one will make him afraid. I pray Pastor will not worry about anything; instead, he will pray about everything. I pray he will tell YOU, God, what he needs, and thank YOU for all YOU have done. If he does this, he will experience YOUR peace, which is far more wonderful than the human mind can understand. I praise YOU, that YOUR peace will guard his heart and mind as I pray he will live in YOU, Christ Jesus.

24. $\mathcal{R}$ EPENTANT:

1 JOHN 1:7-8; ROMANS 8:13-14
AND JAMES 5:16, 19

I pray Pastor will live in the light of YOUR presence, just as Christ is, then he will have fellowship with each other, and the blood of Jesus, YOUR Son, cleanses him from every sin. I pray he will not say he has no sin, as he would be only fooling himself and refusing to accept the truth. For if he kept on following it, he will perish. But I pray Pastor will, through the power of YOUR Holy Spirit, turn from sin and its evil deeds; he will live, because he who is led by the Spirit of YOU, God, is a son of YOU. I pray also that Pastor will confess his sins to each other and pray for each other so that he may be healed. I praise YOU that the earnest prayer of we who pray for him, and of he — a righteous person has great power and wonderful results.

25. SERVANT:

PSALM 86:2-7; EPHESIANS 3:7-8
AND 2 CORINTHIANS 6:4-7, 10

I pray YOU will protect Pastor for I pray he will be devoted to YOU. I pray YOU will always save him, for I pray he will always serve YOU and trust YOU. YOU are his God. Be merciful, O, LORD, for I pray he will be calling on YOU constantly. Give him happiness O, LORD, for his life depends on YOU. O, LORD, YOU are so good, so ready to forgive, so full of unfailing love for all, and he, who I pray, will ask YOUR aid. Listen closely to his prayers. O, LORD, hear his urgent cries. I pray he will call to YOU whenever trouble strikes and YOU, I praise, PROMISE, YOU will answer him. I pray that Pastor will continue to be a servant of YOUR gospel by the gift of YOUR grace given to him through the working of YOUR power. I pray YOU will continue this grace given to him, to preach to the gentiles the unsearchable riches of Christ. And I pray that Pastor, as a servant of YOU, God, will commend himself in every way: in great endurance; in troubles, hardships and distresses; in beatings imprisonment and riots; in hard work, sleepless nights and hunger; in purity, understanding, patience, and kindness; in YOUR Holy Spirit and in sincere love; in truthful speech and in YOUR power, God; with weapons of righteousness in his right hand and in his left; sorrowful, yet always rejoicing; poor, yet making many rich; having nothing, and yet possessing everything.

26. THANKFUL:

COLOSSIANS 3:15-17; 2:6-7

And now, just as Pastor accepted YOU, Christ Jesus, as his Lord, I pray he will continue to live in obedience to YOU. I pray he will let his roots grow down into YOU and draw up nourishment from YOU, so he will grow in faith, strong and vigorous in the truth that he has been taught. I pray his life will overflow with thanksgiving for all YOU have done. And I pray he will let the peace that comes from YOU, Christ, rule in his heart. For as members of one body he is called to live in peace. And I pray he will always be thankful. I pray he will let the words of YOU, Christ, in all their richness, live in his heart and make him wise. I pray he will use YOUR words to teach and counsel. I pray he will always sing psalms and hymns and spiritual songs to YOU, God, with a thankful heart. And I pray whatever he does or says, let it be as a representative of YOU, Lord Jesus, all the while giving thanks through YOU to God the Father.

27. UNDERSTANDING:

**JEREMIAH 33:3; ISAIAH 11:2; COLOSSIANS 1:9-10
AND ROMANS 15:5, 13-14**

I pray Pastor will always ask YOU and I praise YOU, that YOU will tell him some remarkable secrets about what is going to happen here. And I pray for him, that the Spirit of YOU, LORD, will rest on him —YOUR Spirit of wisdom and understanding, YOUR Spirit of counsel and might, YOUR Spirit of knowledge and the fear of YOU, LORD. So I have continued praying for him ever since we first heard about him. I pray for him, asking YOU, God, to give him a complete understanding of what YOU want to do in his life, and I ask YOU to make him wise with spiritual wisdom. Then the way he lives will always honor and please YOU, LORD, and I pray he will continually do good, kind things for others. All the while I pray he will always learn to know YOU, God, better and better. May YOU, God, who gives endurance and encouragement, give Pastor a spirit of unity among us as he follows YOU, Christ Jesus, so that with one heart and mouth we may glorify YOU, God, and Father of our Lord Jesus Christ. May YOU, God of hope, fill him with all joy and peace, as he trusts in YOU, so that he may overflow with hope by the power of YOUR Holy Spirit. I pray he will be full of goodness, complete in knowledge and competent to instruct one another.

28. *V*ICTORY:

PSALM 20:1-5; 37:39-40; JOSHUA 1:5,7;
2 CORINTHIANS 9:8-11; 10:3-5

May YOU, LORD, answer Pastor when he is in distress; may YOUR name of the God of Jacob protect him. I pray YOU will send him help from the sanctuary and grant him support from Zion. May YOU remember all his sacrifices and accept his burnt offerings. May YOU give him the desires of his heart and make all his plans succeed. We will shout for joy when he is victorious and will lift up our banners in YOUR name of our God. May YOU, LORD, grant all his requests. The salvation of Pastor, the righteous comes from YOU, LORD; YOU, I pray, are his stronghold in times of trouble. YOU, LORD, I pray, will help him and deliver him; YOU deliver him from the wicked and save him, because, I pray, he will always take refuge in YOU. I praise YOU that no one will be able to stand up against Pastor all the days of his life. As YOU were with Moses, so YOU will be with him; YOU PROMISE YOU will never leave him nor forsake him. I pray he will be strong and very courageous. May he be careful to obey all the laws YOUR servant Moses gave us, I pray he will not turn to the right or to the left, that he may be successful wherever he goes. And YOU, God, are able and I pray YOU will make all grace abound to Pastor, so that in all things at all times, having all that he needs, he will abound in every good work. As it is written, "YOU have scattered abroad YOUR gifts to the poor; YOUR righteousness endures forever." Now YOU who supplies seed to the sower and bread for food, I pray, YOU will also supply and increase his store of seed and will enlarge the harvest of his right-eousness. I pray he will be made rich in every way so that he can be generous on every occasion, and through us his generosity will result in thanksgiving to YOU, God. For though Pastor lives in the world, he does not wage war as the world does. The weapons he fights with are not the weapons of the world. On the contrary, they have YOUR divine power to demolish strongholds. I pray he will demolish argu-ments and every pretension that sets itself up against the knowledge of YOU, God, and I pray he will take captive every thought to make it obedient to YOU, Christ.

29. *W*ORSHIP:

ROMANS 12:1-2; 15:30-33; JOHN 4:23B-24;

DEUTERONOMY 6:5; 10:12-13 AND PSALM 29:2

I pray that Pastor will, in view of YOUR mercy, offer his body as a living sacrifice, holy and pleasing to YOU, God. This is his spiritual act of worship. I pray he will not conform any longer to the pattern of this world, but be transformed by the renewing of his mind. Then he will be able to test and approve what YOUR will is —YOUR good, pleasing and perfect will. I pray YOU will urge me and my brothers, by YOU, our Lord Jesus Christ, and by the love of YOUR Spirit, to join him in his struggle by praying to YOU, God, for him. I pray that Pastor may be rescued from the unbelievers in Judea and that his service in Jerusalem may be acceptable to the saints there, so that by YOUR will, God, he may come to us with joy and together with us I pray he will continually be refreshed. I pray YOU, God of peace, be with him. And I pray that Pastor will be a true worshiper, who will worship YOU in spirit and truth, for they are the kind of worshipers that YOU, Father, seek. YOU, God, are spirit, and YOUR worshipers must worship in spirit and in truth. And I pray, LORD, that Pastor will love YOU, his God, with all his heart and with all his soul and with all his strength. I pray that he will always do as YOU ask of him to fear YOU, LORD our God, to walk in all YOUR ways, to love YOU, to serve YOU, the LORD our God, with all his heart and soul, and to observe YOUR commands and decrees that YOU give him this day for his own good. I pray he will ascribe to YOU, LORD, the glory due YOUR name, always worshiping YOU, LORD, in the splendor of YOUR holiness.

30. *Y*OUR WORD:

2 TIMOTHY 4:2, 5-6, 17-18, 22
AND PROVERBS 4:20-23; 7:1-5

I pray Pastor will effectively preach YOUR Word; I pray he will be prepared in season and out of season; and I pray he will correct, rebuke and encourage —with great patience and careful instruction. I pray he will always keep his head in all situations, and endure hardship, and I pray he will do the work of an evangelist, I pray he will discharge all the duties of his ministry. I pray YOU, LORD, will stand at his side and give Pastor strength, so that through him YOUR message might be fully proclaimed and all the Gentiles might hear it. And I pray he will be delivered from the lion's mouth. YOU, LORD, I pray, will rescue him from every evil attack and will bring him safely to YOUR heavenly kingdom. To YOU be glory forever and ever. Amen. And I pray that YOU, LORD, will always be with his spirit. And Grace, I pray, will be with him. I pray Pastor will always pay attention; he is YOUR child, to what YOU say. I pray he will listen carefully. I pray he will not lose sight of YOUR words. I pray he will let them penetrate deep within his heart, for they bring life and radiate health to him, who discovers their meaning. Above all else, I pray he will guard his heart, for it affects everything he does. And I pray Pastor will follow YOUR advice; he is YOUR son. I pray he will always treasure YOUR commands. I pray he will obey them and live! I pray he will guard YOUR teaching as his most precious possession. I pray he will tie them on his fingers as a reminder. I pray he will write them deep within his heart. I pray he will love wisdom like a sister, and make insight a beloved member of his family. I pray he will let them hold him back from an affair with an immoral woman, and from listening to the flattery of an adulterous woman.

31. $\mathscr{Y}$EALOUS:

ROMANS 12:9-16, 21; 13:13-14;
MATTHEW 28:18-20; PROVERBS 23:17-18
AND HEBREWS 10:22-23

I pray that Pastor's love will be sincere. I pray he will hate what is evil; clinging to what is good. I pray he will be devoted to one another in brotherly love, honoring another about himself. I pray Pastor will never be lacking in zeal, but will always keep his spiritual fervor, serving YOU, Lord. I pray that he will be joyful in hope, patient in affliction, and faithful in prayer. I pray he will share with YOUR people who are in need and practice hospitality. I pray he will always bless those who persecute him; bless and, I pray, not curse. I pray he will rejoice with those who rejoice, mourn with those who mourn, and live in harmony with one another. I pray he will not be proud, but be willing to associate with people of low position. I pray he will not be conceited. I pray Pastor will not be overcome by evil, but overcome evil with good. Let him always behave decently, as in the daytime, not in orgies and drunkenness, not in sexual immorality and debauchery, not in dissension and jealousy. Rather, I pray he will clothe himself with YOU, Lord Jesus Christ, and he will not think about how to gratify desires of his sinful nature. Then YOU, Jesus, came to them and said, all authority in heaven and on earth has been given to YOU. Therefore I pray Pastor will, in YOUR POWER, go and make disciples of all nations, baptizing them in the name of the Father and of YOU, the Son, and of the Holy Spirit, and I pray he will always teach them and us to obey everything YOU have commanded us. And may he KNOW surely YOU are with him always, to the very end of the age. I pray Pastor will not envy sinners, but always continue to fear YOU, LORD. For surely he has a future ahead of him; his hope will not be disappointed. Let Pastor draw near to YOU, God, with a sincere heart in full assurance of faith, having his heart sprinkled to cleanse him from a guilty conscience and having his body washed with pure water and let him hold unswervingly to the hope he professes, for YOU who promised is faithful!

IN JESUS' PRECIOUS
and POWERFUL NAME...
AMEN!

DAILY REFLECTIONS

REQUESTS

_____
_____
_____
_____
_____
_____
_____
_____
_____
_____
_____
_____
_____
_____
_____
_____
_____
_____
_____
_____

PRAISES

_____
_____
_____
_____
_____
_____
_____
_____
_____
_____
_____
_____
_____
_____
_____
_____
_____
_____
_____
_____

DAILY REFLECTIONS

REQUESTS

_____

_____

_____

_____

_____

_____

_____

_____

_____

_____

_____

_____

_____

_____

_____

_____

_____

_____

_____

_____

PRAISES

_____

_____

_____

_____

_____

_____

_____

_____

_____

_____

_____

_____

_____

_____

_____

_____

_____

_____

_____

_____

DAILY REFLECTIONS

REQUESTS

_____

_____

_____

_____

_____

_____

_____

_____

_____

_____

_____

_____

_____

_____

_____

_____

_____

_____

_____

_____

PRAISES

_____

_____

_____

_____

_____

_____

_____

_____

_____

_____

_____

_____

_____

_____

_____

_____

_____

_____

_____

_____